Roger Griffin

Virginia, 1935

INDIAN SUMMERS

A MEMOIR OF FORT DUCHESNE
1925-1935

BY

VIRGINIA CARLSON PARKER

Logan, Utah
1998

Indian Summers: a Memoir of Fort Duchesne
by Virginia Carlson Parker

Copyright © Virginia Carlson Parker 1998
First printing

Parker, Virginia Carlson, 1923-
        Indian Summers: a Memoir of Fort Duchesne,
        1925-1935. Logan, Utah / Virginia Carlson Parker, -- 1st ed.
        p.: illus., diagr.;   cm.
        Includes bibliography.
        LCCN: 98-072415
        ISBN: 1-888106-4-1

        1. Fort Duchesne (Utah)—History. 2. Uintah and Ouray Reservation.
        3. Parker, Virginia Carlson, 1923-. I. Title.

        920P243   CT275.P3.A3 1998

Portions of "The Experiment Farm" were first published in the Utah State Historical Society *Quarterly*, v. 46, no. 4, Fall, 1978; and Beehive *History* 9. They are reprinted with permission of the Society.

The author is aware of the preference for "Native Americans," rather than using the words "Indians" "braves" or "squaws." Where possible, these changes have been made in this story. Some phonetic spellings of spoken words have been used. Please understand that this is an historical document, set in the period when certain words were in common usage. The use of such terminology implies no disrespect.

Back Cover photo courtesy of Utah State Historical Society

Cover design John Barnhill

Professionally produced
in the United States of America by

800 360-5284
www.agreka.com

I dedicate this memoir to
those who shared the adventures
and to my children who listened
to the stories.

Table Of Contents

EPILOGUE: ABOUT INDIANS

INTRODUCTION

After my mother died, there was no one left in my family with whom I could reminisce about the decade we lived at Fort Duchesne. My brother Leroy, who shared those years with us, died during World War II. It occurred to me to write about those years on the Uintah and Ouray Reservation, so that they could be preserved in the memory of the family. Though I told these stories many times, writing them has been an adventure in self discovery that revealed a significance to the events that I had not suspected. I also believe they are an important part of local history and folklore that needs to be documented.

Autobiographical writing about childhood memories falls somewhere between history and fiction. Selecting experience that can be recounted in an interesting manner results in a somewhat fictional account of historical facts. A memoir of childhood is not free from the influence of adult experiences and perspective. Therefore, writing the history of my personal past has necessitated adding information acquired outside of my personal memory.

As a life long reader of autobiographical writing, I learned that men and women choose a different pattern to recount their lives. Men usually present their life as an orderly process, progressing toward the achievement of a goal, or career. Women record those same events that have had significant influence on their own growth and understanding of themselves in relation to others. Women write about mentors and teachers.

In keeping with this pattern, I have written this memoir as a collection of essays and stories about real events and people, that affected me. I have augmented my memory with historical research to verify what I remembered. I added editorial comments to give meaning to a world that no longer exists. Many of the people I have written about are no longer living, yet they were important to the development of a community that still exists. In writing about the persons who served as my mentors, I added biographical information in order to document their history, as well as mine. Rather than a narrative of sequential events over a decade, I chose experiences that were significant to my growth and development. I present those events as experienced by the child I was. Often the events of several summers merge into one remembered image, and separation has not always been possible. Therefore, I present the stories as the events of one long summer. The stories really happened, and I have used real names of the people who shared them with me. I have added fictional dialogue to create stories that convey folklore in a more dramatic way than prose narrative ever could.

Some of my experiences were unique among my peers. They were unique even in my own family, because my surviving sisters did not share most of them. My sister, Lorraine, was too young; my sister, Nancy, was not yet born. This account of the decade of summers from 1925 to 1935, is also prompted by rapid change and a greatly increased population of the Uintah Basin. A knowledge of the past is necessary to form an understanding of the present.

During my childhood, my family migrated each winter and summer between two worlds of contrasting scenery, values, and experience. As a child I was unable to reconcile conflicts which resulted from those contrasts. I was often squelched by older members of our extended family, who were disinterested and impatient with a child's stories. I was often hurt by wintertime schoolmates, who did not want to share my experience of a place unknown to them.

After we moved permanently to Logan, I ceased talking about my previous experiences and stories because I wanted acceptance from my peers. I became integrated into the life we lived in Logan, and the events of Fort Duchesne were replaced by different activities and concerns. But I never forgot Fort Duchesne, for it remained the home of my childhood. At Fort Duchesne I gained awareness of the world. The most vivid memories were of the *Indians,* my childhood home, and the natural world that surrounded it. Those are the images that inspired my stories. My Memoir is an attempt to preserve those events and people which remain uniquely mine.

Many years have passed since the events that I have written about occurred. In the period of my Memoir there were far more Native Americans than Whites living in the Basin. The population of the Basin is greatly changed. There have been changes in attitudes, also. Native Americans no longer wish to be called Indians. When writing in my own voice, I have used Native American in this Memoir, except in a few places where memory, image, and emotion indicated preference for the word *Indian*. In my essays about Mildred Miles Dillman and Phoebe Litster I have used Indian, because that was the word in use in their time, and the word they used when I interviewed them. I did not change their use of the word *Indian* when I quoted them, or paraphrased what they said, when they told me about their experience with the Utes.

I am grateful to those whose stories I tell and to those who shaped and influenced my understanding of those events. I wish to acknowledge those who consented to an interview after so many years had passed. I value the comments of several historians who read earlier versions of these stories and encouraged me to continue writing them. With gratitude, I acknowledge the assistance of those who have given editorial and technical assistance in preparing this memoir for publication, most especially William Lowry for help with photographs. One folklorist said to me, "It is powerful stuff to remember this in first person. But, when you played games and when you sang songs, what did you play? And what did you sing?" I have included those games and some of the songs. I am grateful to my own children, who first listened to these stories.

This Memoir is for My Family—all of them!

Note: Spelling varies. Uintah is used for civic names.
Unita is used for geographic features.

PROLOGUE

RED ROCK COUNTRY

The red rock country of my childhood was unlike any place I have known since. The sun shone so brightly that it sang. Mysterious red rocks stood up against the sky, casting long grotesque shadows. The rocks were formed in an ancient inland sea, then lifted and exposed. They were carved by the wind and piled like scattered toys abandoned by some forgotten giant.

My experience of the Uintah Basin was like entering an enchanted land in a dream. Each summer we left the fertile green Cache Valley, passed the fruit farms north of Salt Lake City, climbed up through the winding canyons of the Wasatch, crossed over Strawberry Summit, and then descended through a forest of juniper and sand which gradually changed color as we progressed. At first the pink sand was streaked with a chocolate brown, then the pink became darker, and soon red rocks began to appear. After we crossed the Duchesne River, the road emerged into the vast Uintah Basin.

The basin-shaped valley stretches between the Wasatch Range on the west and the Colorado Rocky Mountains on the east. To the north, the valley is backed by the wall of the Uinta Mountains with snow-capped peaks that rise above 13,000 feet. From them, the valley spreads southward until it drops abruptly into the deep canyons of the Green and Colorado rivers. The valley is drained by the Uinta and Duchesne rivers which flow from the Uintas as tributaries of the Colorado River. Green trees, growing in their flood plain, mark their course southward.

During the decade of summers that I lived in the Uintah Basin, it was a landscape almost empty of settlement. Its twenty-five thousand acres held a population of twenty thousand people. Distances were great. Days were long.

Hours were measured by the relentless movement of the sun across a wide, blue sky that was more visible than the land. Each day began suddenly, marked by a series of events that occurred with dependable regularity. As sunlight flared across the desert from the eastern horizon, birds and farm animals joined in a chorus of summery sounds. Overhead, the sky lay unpolluted by smoke, industry, or automobiles. Clouds formed over the peaks of the mountains and were piled like bolls of cotton against the blue sky. Occasional chunks of cloud broke off, and floated over the valley like a regatta of racing sailboats on an endless blue sea.

As the sun climbed upwards, it poured heat onto the bare-bones landscape, baking the tumbled rocks that cast long shadows in which lizards and tiny mammals found shelter from the blistering sun. The least footstep sent them scurrying into the cracks and crevices.

Over time, the wind had carved the sandstone mesas into grotesque forms, boring holes and caves into the pink and chocolate colored cliffs. Breezes shook the sparse blue sage and mesquite, sending their pungent scent to the furthest border. Ancient floods cut deep gullies in the valley floor. The valley floor was so dry and parched that a single thunderstorm could send a torrent roiling through the narrow channels, gathering everything into a flood of muddy water. In the flat areas of the valley floor, placid irrigation canals dug with geometric rectitude, carried water in small streams from the rivers to the fields of alfalfa. The cultivated green fields were strewn across the plateau like a patchwork quilt spread over the desert. Alfalfa cooled the dry air, and perfumed it with the scent of grass. Willow and buffalo berries bordered the canals which served as arteries for the life-giving water that sustained the settlers in that sparsely settled land.

Red dirt roads followed the waterways and linked the scattered settlements to each other. Traffic was sparse. The most common vehicle was a horse-drawn wagon. The few cars and trucks stirred up small dust storms as they sped along their way, making them visible for miles. Old Indian trails formed a less visible network of footpaths beneath the cottonwoods which grew along the river banks.

On the scattered homesteads, lonely houses built of weathered logs, with unpainted doors and window sills, stood in the dusty dooryards that were bereft of lawn or flowers. Barns, chicken houses and round metal granaries were clustered between the house, and the irrigated fields. Young orchards graced some of the farms. The fields were worked with teams of horses. Milk cows gathered in the sparse shade of willows growing along the irrigation ditches bordering the pastures. Horses grazed in fields of native bunch grasses dotted with prickly pear cactus. On most farms, an extended dooryard was planted with vegetables. The gardens were tended by women wearing faded cotton dresses and sunbonnets.

Native Americans camped beside the canals that provided water for their cooking, drinking, and bathing. Their camps included a tepee set under the trees. Shawl-clad women worked communally, laughing and talking while seated in colorful clumps like flowers in the sagebrush. They prepared food, cooked over open fires, wove baskets and worked at bead looms while they tended their small children. Laundered clothes were spread raggedly over the willows to dry. Each camp had a wagon with one or two horses tied to the trees, with several dogs laying nearby. There were many such camps along the canals near the Fort, and in the river bottom. They were within walking distance of the commissary and Administration building. Wong Sing maintained a campground near his trading post where Native Americans camped regularly. White children were not allowed to enter the camps unless invited. We felt estranged, and watched the inhabitants surreptitiously as we passed by while hiking in the nearby hills and along the river bottom.

The Uinta River was a large wild river that flowed in a big bend around the Fort. In early spring, it roared angrily with whole trees tumbling in its current like twigs. The metal bridges trembled and shook above the raging flood. The river dried up in late summer, leaving sand bars and deep pools connected by ribbons of water. The water barely trickled between the pink and gray striped stones that had tumbled from the high Uintas. The river stones were striped because they had once been layers of oil shale and sand that had formed in the ancient sea before it was lifted, and eroded to become the whole Colorado Plateau.

On the sand bars, trees marooned by the springtime floods, were bleached in the dry desert air. Their tangled roots were alive with chipmunks and small lizards. The wood was polished by the wind and sun until it shone like pewter. The river bottom was more than a mile wide, and it smelled of nettles, Indian tobacco, rushes, burdock, buffalo berries, willows, and cottonwoods. Water collected in pools between the sand bars. Some of the pools were deep enough for swimming. In late summer, clouds of gnats, flies and mosquitos swarmed over the tepid water. Bees buzzed on the thistles and herbs that grew among the islands of sand. Native American families camped in tents, or tepees pitched in the shade of the trees that grew along the river bank. They stabled their horses in the small log cabins built for them when Fort Duchesne was established, in 1883. The Fort was built on the high bluff above the river. There, the old barracks stood in a semicircle, shaded by rows of cottonwoods planted by the soldiers.

As the sun descended toward evening, the air cooled, and a soft breeze arose from the river bottom. Leaves of the cottonwoods whispered softly as the air moved through them. The sun slipped behind the western hills, shadows lengthened, and light faded slowly from the evening sky leaving a long twilight before dark. Day ended as the evening star appeared, soon followed by millions of other stars that twinkled in the black night sky. The moon rose from the dark river bottom where crickets, night birds, and coyotes sang their songs. Sometimes the Native American drums sent their sounds into the darkened landscape. Across the valley there were no electric street lights. Lamplight from the windows of the few settlements did not penetrate the darkness very far. Beyond shelter, the night held the promise of mystery and adventure.

Our bedtime began with a warm bath, a glass of milk and a bedtime story. My brother and I shared an upstairs bedroom which had two windows. One overlooked the lawn between the houses and the other overlooked the trees and road that marked the edge of the Fort, separating the Fort from the dark river bottom. Beyond the houses and trees, the desert and hills spread out beneath the starry sky. I never went to sleep without a long look at that dark horizon, which was like a broad stage waiting for the curtain to rise.

If we carry a landscape within us, where memory resides, mine is a wide-open land with large rivers, rainbow hills of red rocks, a long horizon of distant mountains with snow capped peaks, and over all, a wide blue sky. It is a wondrous world of beauty, nearly empty of settlement. It is a land of pioneers and *Indians*. It is a fantasy land I once knew in childhood and only in summer.

EARLY YEARS

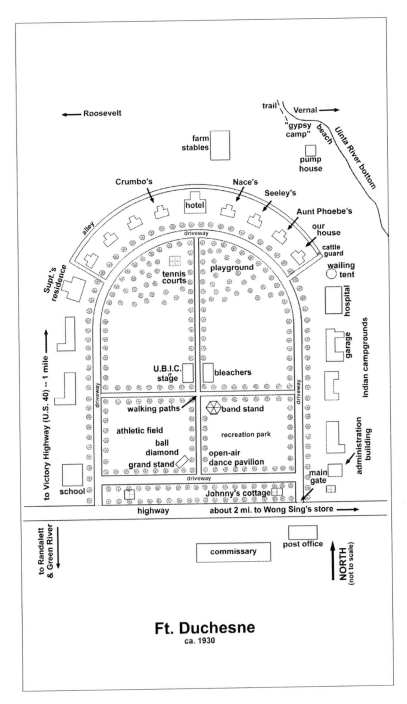

Diagram of Fort Duchesne

Mama, Leroy, Virginia

THE JOURNEY

Round and round went the wheels of my father's new Model T Ford. Gravel spattered against the fenders, as he made his way eastward into the sunrise and the mountains. My first journey to the Uintah Basin was made when I was six months old, in June, 1924. My father had been hired to teach in the High School at Roosevelt. During the summer he traveled through Uintah and Duchesne Counties for the Utah State Agricultural Extension Service, identifying "noxious weeds" that were infecting the alfalfa fields. He had just received his baccalaureate degree in agronomy from the Utah State Agricultural College, and had accepted the teaching position before beginning his graduate studies.

When the Native American lands in the Uintah Basin were opened to White settlement in 1905, it was Utah's last frontier. White homesteads and Native American allotments were scattered in a checkerboard pattern throughout the valley. A network of roads and canals connected the small settlements. The two major towns were the old settlement of Ashley (renamed Vernal) in Uintah County, and Roosevelt in Duchesne County, which was founded when the reservation was opened to homesteading. The headquarters of the combined Uintah and Ouray Reservation was established at Fort Duchesne, which lay midway between the two towns. They were located on a new highway that connected Salt Lake City and Denver. There was little else in the valley to show that it was occupied.

During that first year, my parents established themselves in the basin community, forming friendships with the pioneer families that would last a lifetime. In many ways their association with the Miles, Edwards, Dillman, Orser and Smith families were more satisfactory than any they would ever find again.

When the Uintah Basin Alfalfa Seed Experimental Farm was

established at Fort Duchesne, in 1925, my father was appointed Superintendent of the farm. My family moved to quarters at the Agency and began the twice-yearly migrations which would continue for the next ten years. My father did his field work during the summer at the farm, and his laboratory work at the college in Logan during the winter. This meant moving his family between two homes summer and winter. The geography and culture of the Basin, and the small city of Logan, represented two different worlds. One world was primitive, having been opened to White settlement less than two decades before. Much of it was still a desert of red rocks, sage brush and sand. The other world, a small city of fourteen thousand people located in the most fertile valley in Utah was civilized. In Logan, the streets and sidewalks were paved, and lined with mature trees. The neat rows of houses were set among flower and vegetable gardens with neatly mowed green lawns. The amenities included a large business district, mills and factories, beautiful churches, schools, parks, and playgrounds. Both a tabernacle, and a temple had been built to serve the largely Mormon population. The temple stood prominently on the hill overlooking the valley. The extensive college campus lay next to the mountains.

Most of the settlers in the Basin were Mormon. However, at the Agency where employees of the Bureau of Indian Affairs came from many parts of the United States, a wide variety of religious denominations and cultural experience were represented. I learned very early to be tolerant of persons whose belief was different from that of my parents, including the Native Americans. I also formed opinions that were in conflict with the orthodoxy of my extended family and my wintertime classmates and peers. This made me different, and I grew up with feelings of insecurity, and a determination to define my own belief.

Moving so often meant having two separate sets of friends and schoolmates. My parents' friends, who lived in Roosevelt, became honorary aunts, uncles, and cousins. My grandparents lived in Logan, as did several of my parents' brothers and sisters. The homes of relatives, who lived in Farmington and Lehi, became the stopping places on our journeys to and from Fort Duchesne. Due to the primitive roads, the journey from Logan to

Fort Duchesne usually took two days. We stayed with family to avoid driving in the mountains at night. This also allowed one or two days to shop for supplies in Salt Lake City.

The roads through the mountains were unpaved and seldom traveled. Beyond Price, which was located on the west side of the mountains, there were no motels, or gasoline stations, until we reached Roosevelt, located more than a hundred miles eastward. The little Model T Ford was not made for the primitive conditions of mountain travel, so the journey was always undertaken with some risk. The journey for the family began as soon as snow receded from the mountain passes. My father made frequent stops to allow the engine of his small car to cool, to remove rocks from the roadway and sometimes to repair tires. We stopped by the roadside to eat the lunch we carried with us. As I grew older, the journey became something of an event.

They were interesting journeys, because my father had studied the botany, wildlife, and geology of the country we traveled through. He taught us to observe, and be aware of, the many changes in the landscape. He explained everything, including the miles of snow fences that were stretched across the open fields to keep the snow from drifting onto the road during winter storms. He was familiar with the history of exploration and settlement of the area we drove through, and recounted the stories about them as we passed points of interest. Through the years, we explored every possible route through the mountains.

The road we traveled from Salt Lake City was improved, but unpaved. Only recently completed, as part of the interstate Highway 40, it was grandly labeled the "Victory Highway," in honor of the late World War. Most of its miles were gravel, hardened mud, or red sand. From Heber City, the road followed the old military trail. It wound through Daniel's Canyon, then circled around Strawberry Reservoir where it finally reached the summit. It began its descent through a wilderness of sand and juniper, curiously called Fruitland. After crossing the Duchesne River, it emerged into the vast Uintah Basin. At Myton, the road turned northward toward the Uinta Mountains. We always paused briefly in Roosevelt, to refuel and to greet old friends. Fort Duchesne was another ten miles eastward.

Our arrival at Fort Duchesne was always a joyous climax to the long journey. I am sure that my father turned into the Fort with relief, but for me the anticipation of the summer's adventures was almost unbearable. I could hardly wait to get to my friends from whom I had been separated for an entire winter and school year.

Fort Duchesne was located a mile south of the highway on the western bank of the Uinta River. At the crossroads, stood a rodeo ground backed by a low range of hills. The Fort was visible only as a large grove of green trees growing beneath a bluff

Entrance Gate

of red rocks, and it was approached from the rear. The buildings and main gate faced toward the south, overlooking a plateau that stretched beyond the mesa toward the Green River.

A white picket fence surrounded the once stockaded Fort. Over the entrance gate was a curved arch supported by wooden towers. It bore a sign which read:

FT. DUCHESNE
UINTAH & OURAY INDIAN AGENCY

Suspended beneath was a smaller notice:

This Is Government Property
Those of Orderly Conduct are
Welcome. All Others Stay Out.

The unpaved road crossed a cattle guard beneath the sign, then swung in an arc around a large grass parade. The grass was crisscrossed with walkways, and shaped like a large letter "D" with a straight road across the bottom. Wooden buildings of varying sizes faced the parade ground within the circle of the road. Towering over the buildings were a double row of cottonwood trees which spread leafy limbs to form an arcade. To the right of the entrance stood the Administration Building. It was the largest building at Fort Duchesne. It was built of wood with a high stone foundation. A veranda, supported by stone pillars, stretched across the front. Other buildings included a post office, a commissary, a hospital, several low barracks converted to other uses, a school house, a garage and a row of two story houses. Several small cottages, used to house Native American personnel who worked for the U.S. Bureau of Indian Affairs, were located in a straight line between the entrance gate and the school house, forming the bottom of the "D" shaped Fort.

Ten identical two-storied buildings, separated by wide lawns, stretched around the upper curve. Each building was divided into pairs of identical apartments with screened porches across the front and sides of the buildings. Wooden sidewalks led from an asphalt walk to pairs of double doorways and common steps. Each apartment was half of a former Officer's Barracks. Our apartment was in the end building, next to the hospital.

Residents of Fort Duchesne included both Native American and White employees of the Agency. A few, who worked for other government agencies, were assigned available apartments. A rather large residential hotel, where official visitors and temporary employees stayed, was located in an undivided barracks exactly in the middle of the line of buildings.

The former military post included, within a large circle: a bandstand with a flag pole next to it, a large playground for children, tennis courts, a ball diamond, and the large parade grounds planted with grass. Outbuildings included barns and barnyards, and the pump house, which also served as an ice house and blacksmith shop. A row of garages for automobiles had been built where the stables had originally stood. Immediately behind the houses was an alley lined with woodsheds and garden plots. The alley had a cattle guard at each end with large wooden gates that could be lowered. This allowed a horse drawn wagon to cross over and deliver ice, coal, groceries, or whatever else needed to be delivered to the back entrance of the houses.

Below the Fort was the flood plain of the Uinta River. By 1925, there was little left of the original stockaded fortress. Beyond the tidy, gray buildings was a vast landscape of sandy flatland, sudden arroyos and red rock mesas that stretched southward to the Green River, and north to the Uinta Mountains. The area between was known as the Uintah Basin. Fort Duchesne lay in the very middle of the valley.

My parents always considered Fort Duchesne to be a temporary home because of the nature of my father's work. But for me, it was the only permanent home I knew. Until I was ten years old, we lived in a different apartment each winter, so the Fort was the only place I knew as home.

Traveling is never easy for children, because it means eating strange food, sleeping in strange beds and accepting other makeshift accommodations. All the accommodations had to be accepted with grace and gratitude, difficult virtues for young children to adopt. It could not have been easy for my mother, either, because she had to move all the things her growing family needed for a season from one household to the other. Food, grown and preserved during the summers at the Fort was shifted to Logan for use in the winter. Bedding, clothes, and fabric from which she sewed much of the children's wardrobe, was taken to the Fort for the summer. Those journeys required careful planning, and a great deal of effort. A late spring snowstorm often made the journey very hazardous.

In March 1928, the family nearly met disaster as we were returning to the Basin. Stormy weather turned into a blizzard. My parents had waited two days in Farmington, where they had stayed with Mother's sister, Sena, and her husband, Charles Lloyd. Finally, the weather reports advised that the roads to the Uintah Basin would be passable through the mountains if they remained frozen. According to my father's diary, he left Heber City at midnight, to drive through Daniels and Strawberry Canyons. Near Strawberry Summit, he encountered drifting snow, and was stalled for three hours. The air grew colder as the temperatures dropped, so Father decided to leave Mother, me, and "Baby Leroy" in the car while he walked to the road camp at the summit for assistance.

I remember watching his kerosene lantern fade into the blowing snow as he walked away from us. I can only imagine the fear my mother felt as she reassured us, all the while making a nest from the bedding piled high in the back seat to keep us from freezing. We huddled together in the front seat, wrapped in blankets. She poured what was left of the hot cocoa from the thermos bottle and gave me an oatmeal cookie which I ate with mittened hands.

Snow crystals formed on the windows, and it grew darker. Mama turned out the flashlight and drew us closer. As crystals on the windows and snow obscured the night, she began to sing a familiar lullaby:

> *Oh do you remember a long time ago*
> *When two little babes, their names I don't know*
> *They wandered away on a bright summer day*
> *And were lost in the woods, I've heard people say.*
> *How sad was their plight, how cold was the night.*
> *The sun went down, the moon gave no light.*
> . . .
> *Then the robin so red, brought strawberry leaves*
> *And over them spread. . .*

"Baby Leroy" went to sleep. And I heard Mama pray, "Dear Heavenly Father: Watch over my little ones. Take care of their daddy. Keep them from harm. Don't let us freeze . . ."

Mama's prayer was answered. As dawn broke in the eastern sky, lights of the snow plow appeared through the falling snow. It moved slowly toward us, and we were rescued by the road crew.

In his diary, my father recorded the temperature that night as two degrees below zero. He wrote, "Nearly exhausted by the ordeal, the family arrived at Fort Duchesne at 12 noon, March 16th, sixteen hours after leaving Salt Lake City."

The journey led to new adventures each season. The desert of red rocks, sand, sage brush and alfalfa fields was beautiful and full of promise. Now, if I close my eyes, I hear again the wind in the cottonwoods, crickets in the grass, and from a distant hill coyote calls, and nature is answered by drums in the river bottom, and voices–singing.

SUMMER MORNING

I sat in the empty irrigation ditch near the cattle guard where it curved and widened. The ditch followed alongside the rutted wagon road leading to the barns and stables behind the houses. The ditch's red mud banks were steep and eroded like the arroyos which wound through the desert plateau. The level bottom of the ditch was covered with soft pink sand which I poured from one tin cup to another. A large cottonwood grew on the lawn which formed one bank. Leaning against it, Johnny, my neighbor, sat whittling a piece of cedar with his pocket knife. Marie was busy in the kitchen, so Johnny was watching over me. We spent many mornings like this, saying little.

Virginia, 1927

I was a tow-headed toddler when we moved next door to Johnny and Marie. Our families were assigned living quarters in the same barracks building, remodeled to create two identical apartments. From my earliest memory, Johnny was always there, next door. I played on his screened porch and the shady lawn beside the house as often as I did my own. He taught me many things. He was my friend and brother. Marie helped Mama and tended me. Marie and Johnny were Native Americans, but I did not know it. They were both young and happy, and they had no children. They were exceedingly kind and gentle with me.

Glancing up, I saw slim reeds moving against an azure sky. A dragonfly hovered over them. Its blue-black body bent slightly between gossamer wings as it darted over the stems of grass.

Where the grass grew out of the sand, a lacquered black beetle crept slowly up the bank. It struggled against the sand, rolling grains downwards like loose rocks on the scree of a mountainside.

The ditch was a Lilliputian world filled with diminutive creatures. It hummed with activity. Crickets sang and flies buzzed. The pungent odor of mint contributed to its woodsy smell. Grasshoppers jumped recklessly from one stem to another. A procession of ants, looking like a fleet of miniature black trucks, transported cargo along a wee highway in the grass. A dwarfish green lizard lay motionless on a tumbled boulder, warming in the sun before darting into the cracked mud. A spider had spread her round net between the ragged brown stems of Indian Tobacco. A honey bee landed on the dazzling yellow field of a single dandelion to gather nectar. An orange lady bug flew onto my hand, and walked majestically across the hills and valleys of my knuckles. I blew gently and commanded:

> "Lady bug, lady bug
> Fly away home. . ."

A sudden movement in the weeds brought Johnny to his feet. He quickly snatched a small water snake. "Do not be afraid," he said, draping it over my outstretched hands. The snake's firm muscular body dropped in gray, satiny loops between my hands. The creamy tan scales of its underside flexed and glistened, as it wriggled to be free. I let go. It slid into the long grass and disappeared.

Johnny resumed his whittling. I sprawled on the grassy bank beside him. The earth was cool and hard, and smelled of dampness and decay. Its green surface was mottled with shadows and patches of sun. I pulled a single blade of grass and bit off the tender whitish end. It tasted sweet and crunchy. I chewed the grass stem and watched a robin on the lawn. It ran a few steps, then stopped and cocked its head to listen. It bent and pulled a large red worm from the ground. Ever wary, it flew to a branch of the tree, stopped, looked around, then flew to its nest.

In the grass at the base of the tree lay a hollow blue egg shell. I picked it up and fitted it on my finger like a tiny thimble. I leaned against the tree and listened to the choir of birds. Robins chirruped from their nests. A mourning dove spread its melancholy lament into the morning sunshine. Magpies quarreled from the fence posts. Woodpeckers hammered a quick tattoo against the sunbaked woodshed. A meadowlark's clear notes rippled up from the flower garden. From overhead branches came a mischievous, "Chickadee-dee-dee!"

Far above my head the cottonwood limbs spread broadly across the lawn. Their heart-shaped leaves trembled restlessly in a gentle breeze. They parted ever so slightly, letting bits of blue sky slip through the branches. Wisps of cotton floated in the air like snowflakes, drifting into little white patches at the base of the deeply creased trunk like new fallen snow. The broad trunk cast a long shadow in the morning sunshine. The breeze carried the scent of honeysuckle and roses. Time stood still.

On June 17, 1927, our second summer at Fort Duchesne, Mama sent me to Johnny and Marie's backyard to play. While he watched over me, Johnny sat and whittled while I lolled on the grass. Marie was helping Mama. I felt no anxiety when Dr. Lurrine Miles and Belle Blumer arrived. Dr. Miles was a personal friend and our family physician, who was summoned from Roosevelt. Mrs. Blumer was the practical nurse who came when there was sickness in the house.

When I saw Dr. Miles carrying her black bag into our house, I became alarmed. She hurried into the house, from which I had been excluded. Johnny did his best to divert my attention and to distract me. He finished the willow whistle he had made, and putting it to his lips, he danced across the lawn. I laughed and followed him. Breathless, we dropped onto the grass. Then crawling on hands and knees, we searched for a fourleaf clover.

"Good luck, if you put it in your shoe," he said.

Some time later, Marie came from around the house. Taking me by the hand, she led me upstairs into Mama's bedroom. Mama, wearing her silk dressing gown, lay propped up by pillows. She held a blue bundle in her arms. Reaching out, she drew me close and turned back one corner of the blue bundle and said, "How do you like your new baby brother, John Leroy?"

I studied the wrinkled red face with its tiny mouth and tightly closed eyes. I was puzzled and disappointed. I wanted a playmate. The baby in the bundle began to cry.

Mama did not recover from her confinement for several weeks. "Baby Leroy" developed colitis and became critically ill. Both Mama and "Baby" required special nursing care for a long time. Mrs. Blumer was given my room so she could be near her patients, and my bed was moved downstairs to the sleeping porch. There I slept alone, watching strange shadows on the wall and listening to unfamiliar sounds in the dark. Mama and "Baby" remained upstairs while I was excluded from her room. I did not like the changes.

Dr. Miles came every day and Mrs. Blumer took charge of the house and kitchen. Belle Blumer was a very large woman, efficient and brusk in her manner. Her voice was firm and commanding. I did not like her, because she banished me from my Mama. The changed house had become hushed and shadowed, disturbed only by the crying of the newborn baby. My daddy was worried, and his anxiety made him impatient. Only Marie, who came each day to work in the kitchen and laundry, was unchanged. I clung to Marie for comfort. When she finished with her tasks, she took me to her house to play.

Johnny worked at the Administration building where he served as interpreter for the Agency, so his work hours were irregular. He waited at home to be summoned when needed. I played on their screened porch, or on the shady lawn beside the house. I often ate with them, and sometimes slept there, to avoid disturbing my own household. During those anxious days, Marie sat with me, and sang lullabies to me. Her voice was soft and sweet. When he wasn't busy, Johnny played with me. He pushed me in the swing, lifted me over the cattle guard, and watched while I played in the sand of the irrigation ditch at the edge of their lawn.

Sometime during that summer, I fell off the low couch in our sitting room. I remember the table lamp crashing down with me. Johnny gathered me in his arms and ran with me to the hospital. I had broken my collar bone, so it had to be splinted and bandaged. My arms were pulled back to keep the bone in position, leaving me in an awkward and helpless position. Johnny and Marie lavished their love and concern upon me that fateful summer. They treated me like a sparrow with a broken wing. I learned to love and trust them as family.

31

While I was in their care, Johnny taught me to sit still and listen to bird songs. He taught me to watch them, to notice the patterns and colors of their feathers, and to notice the difference of their tiny eggs. We watched as fireflies danced in the space between the lawn, and the tall grass along the irrigation ditch. I was afraid of the dark, so he taught me to listen to night sounds, to identify them and name them. As it grew dark in the evening, we listened for crickets singing in the shadows, and to a barn owl hooting from the trees. Sometimes we heard a coyote, whose call was answered from the dark beyond the trees and river bottom. When the sounds became familiar, I was no longer afraid.

During those days and nights, Johnny and I became special friends. He called me "Nah'chits" for little girl. He whittled toy animals from the cedar firewood, and then told me stories about them. Half sung and half spoken, his stories were about frogs, beavers, deer and bears. Johnny gave me a pair of moccasins covered with blue beads. They had beaded roses on the toes. I thought the were very beautiful and wore them until I had outgrown them. Much later, he gave me a beaded hat band that was just like his own. I still have the hat band which is worked in a traditional Ute design of red roses on a background of white beads. Though I have never had a black hat, I once wore the band on a leather belt.

Many years later, after I was all grown up, I was asked whether John Victor had a Native American name. I do not know. Everyone called him Johnny. John was a familiar name to me. My grandfather's name was John. My father's name was John, and it was also the name given to my baby brother. From infancy, I knew "My Johnny" as brother too. And as Johnny he remains. If he had another name I never knew it.

When Mama and baby, John Leroy, were well enough to travel, Daddy took us to Farmington to stay with Mama's sister, Aunt Sena. He said that Mama and "Baby" could get the special medical care they needed in Salt Lake City. We stayed with Aunt Sena for the rest of the summer. My cousin, Edith, and I, were given large matching celluloid baby dolls which we dressed in real baby clothes. I remember hearing the train whistle in the night as the steam locomotive passed down below the farm.

Years passed before I realized the importance of the events

Johnny and I shared on the day my brother was born. That day I was thrust from being the center of attention by the new baby. Gradually, I came to understand that boys were more important than girls. And although I was "Big Sister," "Baby Leroy" was a boy. My mother referred to boys as "chosen spirits." Indeed my brother was a chosen spirit. Barely surviving his precarious infancy he developed slowly, and remained smaller than boys his own age. He had a brilliant mind, a keen wit, and a delightful sense of humor. Everyone loved Leroy. He was the pride and joy of my parents. I, too, loved my brother. We shared most of the adventures of our summers together at Fort Duchesne. But it was John Leroy who remained the chosen spirit in our family, for there were no more sons born to my parents.

We became a family after my baby brother was born. I began to think of "we" and "us," rather than "me." My father bought a new car with a front seat and a back seat. The back seat was ours–mine and Leroy's. Gradually, we began to share everything, including the upstairs bedroom and playroom, for the other rooms remained boarded up. I was given a full size bed, and Leroy was moved out of his crib into the child-sized metal bed with side rails that had been mine. We shared a huge toy chest, a play table and two chairs all painted blue. In the middle of the floor was a large braided rag rug made by Grandma Carlson. We played together, and I became "Big Sister." "Big Sister" was a role that carried privileges as well as responsibilities.

My relationship with my parents changed as I became more aware of them and myself as separate persons. If there was another "chosen spirit" in our family, it was Mama. She created our home, and nurtured all of us with sweet patience, determined know-how, honest goodness, and humble faith in God and man. She was an artist, and was sensitive to beauty, design, color, and feelings. Our home reflected Mama's spirit, but Daddy was the head of our family. His work determined who we were; his authority was respected as the law, and it determined what we did. He was a kind man, who was sensitive to others and who required respect for his principles. He was knowledgeable about many things, and he was a kind and patient teacher. He expected us to excel in school, and to perform with integrity while being tolerant of those who were different from ourselves. He was a religious man whose life was devoted to the search for knowledge and wisdom. He expected the same of his family.

Brother John Leroy and I grew up in a peaceful loving home, and our summers were filled with adventures which we shared.

John Leroy

HOME AND GARDEN

We were a happy family. My parents loved and trusted each other. My father enjoyed his work. Mother was proud of her husband, and supported him completely. They cherished their children. Both parents had grown up in large families of modest means. Their parents were immigrants from Scandinavia, and converts to The Church of Jesus Christ of Latter-day Saints. My grandparents reared their families according to the principles of their chosen religion, and reinforced them with values learned in their homeland. Each of my parents had acquired a sincere belief in the values of thrift and industry, native intelligence, integrity, and education. As members of the Mormon Church, my family attended services in the Gusher Ward, which was part of the Roosevelt Stake. Since there was no chapel, we attended Sunday School in the Gusher schoolhouse, just east of Fort Duchesne. Mother served in the Stake Relief Society as an officer and teacher, which allowed my parents to maintain frequent contact with their friends in Roosevelt and Vernal.

Because Mother was often in Roosevelt, I spent much time in the homes of her friends. The women I remember were sisters, daughters of pioneer settlers in the Basin. They were educated in Salt Lake City in various professions. They were married to prominent leaders of the Basin community. They all lived in the same neighborhood. Dr. Lurrine Miles practiced medicine throughout the Basin, and had a small hospital in half of her home. She was physician to my family, because we were not eligible for medical services at the Agency. She was married to Jess Allen. He was a sheep rancher whom we knew as Uncle Jess. Mildred Miles Dillman, whom I called Aunt Bill, was married to Ray Dillman. He was Duchesne County Attorney. He was a director of many civic and charitable organizations in the Basin community, and a prominent landowner. He served as Bishop and Stake President of the Mormon Church in Roosevelt. Mildred Dillman was an anthropologist who studied Ute culture and collected Native American baskets, rugs, and other artifacts. She was a teacher in the Native American school at Whiterocks, and befriended many Native Americans. Martha Miles Edwards "Aunt Mattie" to everyone, was a teacher at Roosevelt High School. She and Mary Orser, were teachers at the High School during the year my father taught there. Mattie was married to Homer Edwards. He was manager of the Ashton store in Roosevelt, and was prominent in the Chamber of Commerce, and other business affairs. All these women were highly educated and active in community affairs. Mildred and Mattie had children my age, so I spent much time in their homes. These women were important role models for me, and had a positive influence in my childhood and development as a person.

My mother was an efficient homemaker who possessed many skills acquired in the pioneer ranch life of her childhood. She was an accomplished seamstress, and had special training in art and interior decoration. She loved flowers, and created a wonderful garden at Fort Duchesne. I became interested in gardens because my mother loved and grew flowers.

My father was an agronomist, and for him plants were the most interesting things in his world. To him there were basically only two kinds of plants "economic plants" and "noxious weeds." Of the former, the prime example was alfalfa. This marvelous plant was the means of earning his living as well as his avocation. For most of his life alfalfa was his chief topic of conversation. He spent his entire working life improving alfalfa plants and their growing conditions. The years at Fort Duchesne were just the beginning of his investigations into the growing of alfalfa, as a crop for seed, as well as for forage.

Alfalfa, which means "the father of all foods," is a plant native to Persia. The Moors carried it across Africa to Spain as fodder for their horses. It is a plant which requires an arid climate and lots of sunshine. The plant thrived in Spain, and was carried to the New World by Spanish Conquistadors when they took their horses to New Spain. Alfalfa was planted in their Mission Colonies by the missionaries, first in Baja California, then in Alta California. Soldiers of the Mormon Battalion, returning to Utah from San Diego, brought alfalfa seeds to Utah and planted them.

On the shores of the Great Salt Lake, alfalfa found a land much like ancient Persia. Alfalfa thrived wonderfully, providing hay for horses and cattle, and means of reclaiming the alkaline and irrigated soils. Alfalfa was an especially valuable crop in the Uintah Basin. Alfalfa provided the best hay, and its blossoms provided nectar for bees. Alfalfa seed and honey were two crops that were economically feasible for this isolated land beyond the mountains, because they could easily be transported to market by wagon and truck.

After about twenty years, the seed crops began to fail. The alfalfa produced flowers and the bees produced honey, but the seed pods failed to produce seed. A disaster was in the making, and no one knew why. In 1925, the Utah State Agricultural Experiment Station established an experimental farm to study the problem and find a solution. The site chosen was near Fort Duchesne and my father was appointed Superintendent. The land was an allotment belonging to a Ute named John Quip, and it was leased for ten years.

The only available housing for the Superintendent's family was at the headquarters of the Uintah and Ouray Indian Agency at Fort Duchesne. That is how we came to call one of the converted barracks home. The barracks were in a bad state of disrepair, having been partially dismantled to obtain materials to repair other buildings. My father had been trained as a carpenter, so with help from the Agency and the Experiment Station, he set about to remodel the old barracks. He had taught at Roosevelt High School the previous winter, so his family remained in Roosevelt until the apartment was finished.

The barracks had neither running water nor electricity, so an ell was added to the building by extending what had been a butler's pantry attached to the dining hall. This was enlarged to accommodate a combined bathroom and laundry, with plumbing for the kitchen sink on the common wall. Electric wires were run along the surface of the walls and ceiling to the two bedrooms upstairs, the three rooms on the ground floor, and in the halls and stairwell.

The former dining room was partitioned off with a three-quarter wall to create a kitchen, and a small sitting room. It was heated by the cooking-stove which was backed by a built-in bookcase.

The sitting room was furnished with a small couch, an upholstered rocking chair for Mama, and another one of oak with a leather seat for Daddy. They shared a reading lamp which sat on a small table specially designed to hold a crystal radio set. On the other side of the partition was the kitchen cabinet, the sink and an ice box. In the corner was a drop-leaf table and chairs. I even remember the pictures on the walls. One was a sepia print of the Greek statue, *The Winged Victory*, that stands on the staircase of the Louvre Museum in Paris. The other was a colored print of Leonardo da Vinci's *The Last Supper.* The table and chairs beneath were painted orange with blue edges. I loved that pretty corner.

What served as the parlor in other apartments was furnished as a dining room in our apartment. We had a matching suite of table and chairs, as well as a china closet. The room had a fireplace that was closed with brick. Its chimney was used by a small heating stove. Over the mantle was a large colored print of a field of wild flowers that my father had brought back from his Mission in Sweden. On the mantle stood a pair of wooden candle sticks and a vase that Mother kept filled with flowers. The screened front porch served as a parlor since the apartment was only occupied during the summer. It was furnished with a chintz-covered day bed, and a pair of wicker arm chairs. A hammock hung cater-corner across the right angle of the porch. The porch railing had been widened to support flower boxes. Mother also had her sewing machine on the porch. The porch extended along the side to the ell, and a portion of the porch was partitioned off to serve as a sleeping porch. The sleeping porch was wall to wall beds that were available to overnight guests.

All rooms opened onto a hallway that extended the full length of the building. Upstairs, two bedrooms and a small dressing room were furnished. The back bedrooms, as well as the third floor attic had been boarded up, and were unused. At the head of the stairs was a large copper fire extinguisher, and beside it my mother kept a huge basket of cut flowers that were visible from the front double doors at the bottom of the stairs. The stairs and hall had bare uncarpeted floors that were stained darker than the bannister. They were polished and shining clean. Paint, wallpaper and colorful curtains made an attractive and colorful home.

On the ground floor, beneath the boarded up rooms, were two additional large rooms which served as kitchen and laundry in the other apartments. In our house, they had no finished floors, just rough sub-floor boards. One room was used as a store room and back porch, because it had a door that opened to the side of the building and served as our back entrance door. It had a six-foot square ice box, shelves for food storage, a long work bench, and a place where Mother did her ironing. One corner of the back room had been finished as a photographic darkroom. The rough floor was covered with rag rugs. The room behind it had no floor at all. It was used as a dirt cellar to store vegetables and batches of root beer.

The landscaping also made our house unique. My father sought advice from the horticulture department he worked with at the Agricultural College. Surrounding our porch were fine specimens of flowering shrubs that provided shade and privacy. They included choice varieties of lilac, honeysuckle and bridal wreath that bloomed in early summer.

Though alfalfa thrilled my father, my mother needed flowers to make her happy. Everywhere she lived, she planted flowers. She loved growing them, and harvesting them as cut flowers. Mother was an artist, and she arranged beautiful bouquets in her vases and baskets. For this purpose, she designed and planted a large flower garden. She entered her flowers in the county fairs and the Uintah Basin Industrial Convention. Over the years, she collected a whole sheaf of ribbons for her prizewinning entries. A picture remains of a blue-ribbon bouquet of Shasta daisies that were arranged in a basket Mama wove herself.

Mama's and Daddy's appreciation of plants differed. When we drove by a field of alfalfa in bloom, I smelled grass and noticed a drop in the temperature of the air. Daddy would exclaim, "What a great set of bloom for seed!" Mama would reply quietly, "What a lovely shade of blue."

One of my earliest memories is that of a bee gathering nectar from a large pink flower. I asked Daddy what it was called. I remember his reply, "The pink flower has the name *alcea rosea*, now use it!" I was standing near the bird bath which stood at the crossing of gravel paths, lined with the pink and white striped boulders carried from the river bottom. A wall of hollyhocks and delphiniums stood behind the bird bath. I was quite small, and felt chastened by my father's curt reply.

The flowers towered over me and they seemed enormous. I preferred my mother's names for the flowers. Behind the border, a hedge of lilacs was planted to screen out the view of the barn-yards. A row of daisies grew along one side of the walk. Large beds of perennial flowers provided Mama with a constant supply of cutting flowers. There were peonies, poppies, larkspur, del-phiniums, nasturtiums, straw flowers, baby's breath, and cosmos. Mama never grew roses. They were too much trouble in the short season we spent at the Fort.

Lorraine, Leroy, Virginia and Mama

Mama's artistic eye always saw the possibility for an artistic design. She had painted flower designs on her trousseau dishes. Besides growing and painting flowers, she embroidered flowers. I remember her teaching me embroidery stitches to add designs to napkins, dish towels, and pillow cases. I liked making the lazy-daisy stitch, which was used to lay flower petals on cloth. It wasn't easy to make the long loop stitch, then take a tiny stitch at the end to tack the petal down. A circle of petals created a daisy flower. After having successfully decorated the corners of dish towels made from flour sacks, I was making a pair of pillow cases for Grandma for Christmas. The border design was a simple chain of pink, blue and yellow daisies. I stitched on percale which was much firmer than muslin. It fit well in the wooden embroidery hoop. Mama made me do the stitches over and over until the flowers lay neatly on the cloth.

Whenever we went on what Daddy called "drives," we explored the world we passed through. He taught Leroy and me how to search the hillsides for wildflowers. Again, there was a difference in my parents. As a botanist, Daddy searched for rare and unique flowers to add to his collection. Mama noticed flower designs and colors. She told us that flowers all had story book names like Indian Paintbrush, Jack-in-the Pulpit, Lady's Slippers, and so on. But Daddy corrected her, saying that each flower had names that identified them everywhere in all the world. Just like me, they had a family name, and a common name that described their form.

Daddy knew all about mountains, valleys, rivers, and rocks. He saw the Uintah Basin as an opportune textbook spread out for us to observe and absorb. As we stood on the high plateaus, and traced the path of the rivers, he explained how mountains were formed, and how rivers cut the valleys. On the canyon sides, he pointed out the different colored layers of sand that had turned into stone, creating the red rock landscape that lay before us.

Hiking among the rocks, we searched for fossils. We found tiny shells imbedded in rocks. We collected stones that were imprinted with skeletons of fish, leaves and ferns. We found rounded stones called "thunder eggs" that were supposed to be the eggs of dinosaurs. We looked for geodes, which had wonderful lavender crystals inside.

Daddy took us to Dry Gulch Canyon to see the petroglyphs. There we saw immense rock walls covered with drawings of giants with square heads and shoulders. There were giant animals, deer, antelopes, spinning wheels and stars. The petroglyphs were wonderful and he took everyone who came to visit us to see the petroglyphs and the dinosaur quarry at nearby Jensen.

Those excursions were exciting adventures. The roads were few, so the turns and bridges over canals and rivers became familiar. Leroy and I named some of the rocks, like the huge red

sandstone rock shaped like a toad that formed the mountain behind Bishop Hacking's turkey farm. Another formation we called
Sugar Loaf was recognized by everyone who went past it on the
way to Wong Sing's store.

Leroy and I spent lots of time together. We did jigsaw puzzles,
played table games, pored over the pages of illustrations in the
Webster's unabridged Dictionary and read stories to each other.
We had a set of *The Wonder World* which were volumes of stories and fairy tales. We cut pictures from magazines to make scrap
books of animals and far away places. Our favorite magazine
was the *National Geographic* which didn't even have colored
pictures at that time. We had a small rotary press with rubber
type, and with help from Daddy's typewriter, we printed a small
magazine that we sold for large safety pins we used to hang blankets on the clothesline for the curtains of our theater. One of the
big events of the summer was a play the children staged on the
lawn between our house and Aunt Phoebe's. Most of August was
spent painting scenery, making costumes and rehearsing our show.
Nearly all the parents attended. Homemade ice cream was served
when the play was over.

Our summers were busy and happy. Our home was peaceful
and orderly. Yet there was always an awareness of another place,
and of other people, of other family. Summers at Fort Duchesne
were unique and wonderful, because they were filled with events
that made us a community. Those events gained importance as I
learned to appreciate the people who shared them with us. Remembering those summers, I came to understand that it was those
events and those people who formed my values, shaped my sense
of self, and made me who I am.

AUNT PHOEBE

Phoebe Lister, ca. 1970

One Monday wash day in June, I hurriedly pinned stockings to the line so I could go to Aunt Phoebe's until lunchtime. I usually hung the socks neatly in pairs, but that day I flung them over the lines like so many magpies on a fence. The clothesline stretched across the lawn that separated our back door from Aunt Phoebe's. I ducked under the sheets, and raced to her side door which opened into the kitchen. Skipping the bottom step, I reached up to knock on her door. I admired the yellow rambling rose that completely covered the porch. I ruffled a cluster of blossoms that hung just above my head, and scattered petals on the doorstep causing a cloud of fragrance that engulfed me.

"Come in, Virginia." Aunt Phoebe called out, having anticipated my coming.

I opened the screen and went in. The aroma of coffee mixed with the scent of roses filled the room. Aunt Phoebe was sitting in her rocking chair beside the wood-burning cooking stove where an enamel coffee pot perked gently. Her apron was filled with peas, which she shelled into a colander. The open oven door spilled heat into the morning sunshine. Loaves of bread, fresh from the oven, cooled on the table. Aunt Phoebe said she drank coffee for her heart, but I believe she really kept the pot ready to share with her visitors as she welcomed them to her kitchen.

"Do you want me to help shell peas?" I asked.

"No, no. Run along, you've little enough time," she said, waving me toward the stairs. "Just close the door, no one will disturb you. Gene won't be back 'til tomorrow."

Gene Louise was my best friend and the baby of her family. The door to which Aunt Phoebe referred led from the upstairs hallway to the attic. It was closed with a latchstring so it could be secured from the inside. What she kept in her attic could only be called a treasure trove. The old magazines that filled the attic was a secret Aunt Phoebe and I shared. Aunt Phoebe had made it my place of refuge.

The attic was partitioned for rooms, but most of the walls had been stripped of their boards and were now unfinished. The doors had been removed to repair other buildings. Near the middle of the largest room, was a large wooden skylight propped open for ventilation. Sunshine poured through the opening, and made a pool of sunlight in the delightfully dusty attic. The bare wooden floor extended under the eaves where there were piles and piles of old magazines. They had been stacked away from the opening so that a sudden shower would not rain on them. The tumbled piles had accumulated for decades. To me, Aunt Phoebe's untidy attic was pure heaven!

Aunt Phoebe's library reflected her insatiable curiosity. The eclectic piles included *Literary Digest, Liberty Magazine, Harpers, Scribners, St. Nicholas, Collier's, Saturday Evening Post, The Delineator, Ladies Home Journal* and assorted Westerns with tattered and yellowed pages. In separate piles, were various magazines published by the L.D.S. Church–*The Women's Exponent, The Young Women's Journal, The Relief Society Magazine and The Children's Friend.* Stacked more carefully were years of the *National Geographic Magazine*, which were endlessly fascinating because of the photographs of far away places I had never imagined. There were also stacks of colored funny papers from the *Denver Post.* During my summers at Fort Duchesne, I spent hundreds of hours in that magazine-filled bower, reading stories that transported me to imaginary lands and adventures of every kind. Stretched out on an old rag rug spread beneath the open skylight, I had my very own magic carpet.

The summer sun poured through the opening, sending rays of dust motes into the shadows. An occasional butterfly flitted in through the opening, fluttered about, and then finding no flowers, left again. Large brown and orange moths hung motionless, on the dusty windows, and spider webs filled the corners, transforming them into stained glass. A breeze carried the smell of cedar shingles baking in the clear desert sunlight. I could hear the distant sounds of a hand-pushed lawn mower, of wood being chopped, of horses clopping down the alley, and of flies buzzing against the window panes. From the barnyards beyond the Fort came other summery sounds of cows and chickens. The sounds were punctuated by occasional shouts of children in the playground across the road. It was a wonderful place for dreaming and imagining. It was my own private bower to which I ascended as often as I could.

Aunt Phoebe guarded the time I spent there, nurturing my reading and fantasizing. We were kindred spirits, Aunt Phoebe and I. Occasionally, when Mama interrupted my day dreams for some prosaic chore, Aunt Phoebe denied knowing where I was, allowing me to finish my stories, and my day dreams. Children need a secret place for dreaming. Aunt Phoebe's attic was my secret place. Its door was always mine to open and to close against the real world.

Though Aunt Phoebe was much older than my mother, to me she was ageless. She was tall and slim. Her blue eyes twinkled from beneath arched brows. She wore her black hair crimped into tiny waves, parted in the middle, pulled back from her high cheek bones, and gathered into a little knot at the back of her head. Her pale skin was powdered, but she wore no rouge or lipstick. Her voice was low and friendly, and her laugh was a pleasant and infectious chuckle. I never remember her being cross, or scolding any child.

Aunt Phoebe was most often found in her kitchen, where she sat in her rocking chair placed next to the stove. Strategically placed, she could see whoever entered any of the four doors which opened onto the kitchen one from the back room and alley beyond, one from the side porch off the kitchen, one from the dining-room, and most importantly, the one from the long hallway with the front door at its end. Beside her stove, Aunt Phoebe held court. Frequent visitors came to see her there. Aunt Phoebe had lived at Fort Duchesne longer than anyone, and she reigned as the undisputed queen of the Fort.

Mama and Aunt Phoebe had long been friends, but to me she was more like a Fairy Godmother. Aunt Phoebe understood the difficulties I had integrating my summer and winter worlds, and she did much to smooth my transitions. She nourished my curiosity and creativity, and she encouraged me to be independent. As we shared our love for reading, and she made her attic a haven for me, she became my first mentor.

I did not learn the facts of her life until many years after we moved away from Fort Duchesne. She visited us in Logan whenever she came to the Extension Service training sessions held at the College. As a child I had taken her for granted, and did not know what her contribution to the community at Fort Duchesne had been. I learned all that when I went to see her after my mother died. By then she was more than ninety years old.

Phoebe Carron Nye was born at Mountain Dell, Utah on August 3, 1881. Her family was among the pioneer Mormons who settled in the Uintah Basin in the early 1860's. She grew up on a homestead in Ashley Valley, and attended school in Vernal. She married a classmate, Campbell Litster. He had immigrated from Scotland at the age of thirteen as a convert to Mormonism. They were married in April 1900.

Campbell Litster entered the Indian Service, and served in Oregon and New Mexico before returning to the Ute Reservation at Fort Duchesne in 1912. He was a jolly and friendly man who never lost his Scottish burr in his voice. He was Maintenance Engineer in charge of maintaining the buildings and grounds at the Uintah and Ouray Agency. He had sandy hair and a burly figure. He was liked by both Native Americans and Whites, and was a pleasant man to do business with. He played an excellent game of tennis which he taught to all the children at the Fort.

The Litster's had seven children. Four of the children were married and gone from home when we came to live next door. Bob, Bill, and Gene Louise remained at home. Gene, who was a year older than I, became my closest friend and playmate. We spent lots of time together for there were no other little girls of our age living at the Fort.

When the Utah State Alfalfa Seed Experimental Farm was established on land that was part of the reservation, my family was assigned living quarters at Fort Duchesne. We moved into the building between Litster's and the Hospital. Mr. Litster helped my father remodel the vacant quarters.

While Mr. Litster served as maintenance engineer, Aunt Phoebe served as the telephone and telegraph operator for the Agency. This put them in a position to know everyone, and most everything that happened in such a small community. Intelligent, curious, and friendly, Phoebe Litster was uniquely qualified to serve as the Fort's communications director. She was active in community affairs, especially as they affected the children. She served The Church of Jesus Christ of Latter-day Saints as teacher and missionary. She worked with the Extension Service of the Utah State Agricultural College in its effort to improve the social life of the employees of the Agency. She was a leader in the Farm Bureau and Extension programs for youth groups, and she had served on the Uintah Basin Industrial Convention (U.B.I.C.) Committee since it began in 1923. She took advantage of every opportunity for self-education, and for volunteering her services to the community. She was an enchanting storyteller, and a born actress which made her an effective teacher. She loved making up games to play. Her absolute favorite entertainment was a picnic. And her picnics included everyone. The most special picnics were those held at what she named the Gypsy Camp. I shall always be grateful that we became neighbors, for I have never known anyone like Aunt Phoebe again throughout my life.

Campbell Litster retired from the Bureau of Indian Affairs in 1936. They moved to Salt Lake City where Aunt Phoebe purchased a small home in Sugar House. She intended to retire there because it suited her to be near the university and members of her family. Campbell Litster was homesick for the Basin. They returned to an apple farm in Ashley Valley where they lived until he died in 1942.

Aunt Phoebe moved back to her home in Salt Lake City. She

worked at the Salt Lake City Public Library until the age of eighty-two, when she retired to the honored ranks of storyteller and grandmother. She continued to plan picnics and reunions of old friends.

I went to see her in June of 1975, when she was nearing her ninety-fifth birthday. I had not seen her since I had gone away to school in 1943. When I entered her parlor she said, "I was just sitting here, remembering all the people I have known and you came." Three decades had passed since I last visited her. I found her frail, but alert as ever. Roses grew on a trellis over her front door. She lived alone, surrounded by photographs of her grand-children, and by stacks of books and piles of magazines. She sat in her rocking chair near the fire place. I sat on a stool in front of her, just like when I was a child. As she shared stories and photo-graphs of her family, she answered my questions. I felt like there had been no passage of time since we were last together.

She told me more about some of the people we had known, and explained some of the things I had been too young to under-stand or inquire about in earlier years. She told me she had first seen Fort Duchesne before there were any buildings. The sol-diers were quartered in tents, and the only trees at the Fort were in the river bottom. She had helped plan the first U.B.I.C., and every subsequent one until they moved away from the Basin. We talked about Wong Sing, Johnny Victor, Mr. Pappas, Grandma Daniels, and others who lived at the Fort. She kept in touch with many of them, and had lived longer than most of them. She re-membered my mother and Leroy with a special fondness. She seemed happy, and at peace with her world.

Aunt Phoebe died in Salt Lake City the following June, in 1976. She had been planning a Bicentennial Picnic, and a re-union of all the Basin families. It was to be held at Liberty Park, on her birthday in August. It would have been her favorite kind of celebration.

Phoebe Litster served an important role in the development of the Uintah Basin, and of Fort Duchesne. She was a link be-tween cultures. She helped Indians and Whites to know and ap-preciate each other. Her mission had been to build bridges be-tween the Gentiles and the Mormons, between the Whites and the Indians, between the old and the young, between settlers and the newcomers, and between the powerful and the powerless. She was called Aunt Phoebe by every child she ever knew, and all were welcome at what she called "The Children's Home."

She succeeded in her calling because she was informed, tolerant, charming, and wise. Aunt Phoebe's greatest gifts to me were love and respect. Her love gave me a self-confidence that helped me bridge the gap between the two worlds of my childhood. And her uncritical acceptance of me helped me find the courage to believe in myself with a desire to achieve. Under her tutelage I gained empathy for the Native American, the Chinese, the Greek, the non-Mormon, and the unschooled. Her respect for my family helped me find pride in my own heritage. Aunt Phoebe will always hold a special place in my heart and memory. Even though her daughter was my playmate, Aunt Phoebe was always my friend, and my mentor. No one in my own family loved me quite like Aunt Phoebe did. It was Aunt Phoebe who informed my *Indian Summers*. I am privileged to have known her. She earned the halo which I saw shining around her head like a wreath of silver hair on our last summer afternoon together.

THE SAND BOX

Daddy built a sand box for Leroy and me in the corner formed by the back steps and the ell. This was no ordinary sand box. It held enough sand to build an entire landscape of valleys, fields, canals, bridges, a "dugway", and a village, with a big garage and gasoline pump for our miniature cars and trucks. Of course it resembled the world we traveled through on our journeys through the mountains from Logan to Fort Duchesne.

The Sand Box Corner
Leroy, Garth and Grant Seeley

The sand box was big enough for three to five children to sit in. Once begun, the landscape developed slowly over the entire summer. We preserved it by covering it when rain threatened–a rare occurrence. It was never vandalized because it was shared by the entire community of children.

The sand came from the river bottom. It was very fine and slightly pink in color. After much experimentation, we discov-

50

ered that if we mixed it with wood ashes and water we could mold it like concrete. So we paved the roads, and built abutments for bridges. On our stops in Salt Lake City, at the Kress store we bought small trucks and cars. They were manufactured in Germany and cast of a soft metal with rubber wheels and parts that moved. Over the years we assembled a whole fleet, and we played with them very carefully. They were not stamped out of plastic and disposable like later toys. They were valuable property.

I don't remember really playing in our small world. As we built the world, we talked it into existence. We collected all sorts of small pieces of lumber and stones to build houses, garages, barns, and bridges. We cut up wooden strawberry boxes, and glued pieces of balsam wood together to construct buildings of various sizes. We whittled pieces of willow to make logs for cabins and corrals. We cut twigs of cottonwood and honeysuckle which we planted in the sand for trees. We painted, and installed road signs made of cardboard. We gathered broken red rocks from the nearby hills to build arroyos and "dugways." Nothing was discarded without first considering how it could be used in the sand box.

Mama's kitchen window overlooked the sand box, so it was convenient for her to keep an eye on us while we played. At one time, Daddy built a fence around the area and hung large orange stenciled signs to warn everyone that we were being quarantined for Whooping Cough. Another time he came home from Roosevelt with a young maple tree in the back of his truck. We dug a deep hole between the corner of the ell and the clothesline, and then planted the tree. I waited and waited for it to grow, expecting it to cast shade over the sand box. Eventually it shaded one corner, but as long as we lived at Fort Duchesne it never grew big enough to hang a swing in it.

I do not know when the sand box was abandoned. Perhaps we outgrew it, or became bored with it. A summer thunderstorm washed most of it away. We repaired the roadways, but never rebuilt the "dugway" and bridges. Eventually Mama raked out the rocks and pieces of wood. The lawn crept in, and as grass will, it quietly covered our make-believe world.

We played other make believe games. A game similar to sand box was played only by the girls. Too sissy for the boys, we called

51

it Trinkets. We collected all sorts of small boxes, bottles, scraps of fabric, and things to build palaces and gardens for small china dolls which we also purchased at the Kress store in Salt Lake City. Our palaces were usually built on the floor of the screened porch. They were tolerated for several days, then carefully packed away into shoe boxes to wait for another game of Trinkets.

Like most little girls, I loved to play dress up. I usually played with Gene, or Aunt Bill's little girls in Roosevelt. Mama was young during the Flapper period, but she didn't wear fashionably exotic clothes. Much to my dismay, she never even wore high heel shoes. I remember raiding her closet upstairs and the most glamorous thing in it was an orange dressing gown embroidered with black Japanese designs. It had a long silk sash, and it was wonderful to wrap oneself in. I loved playing in Mama's bed-room. Her dresser was painted pale green with little sprays of roses made of gesso and painted pink. I thought this was a very glamorous piece of furniture. On top was an ivory dresser set with a hand mirror, tray, powder boxes, and a little round box fitted with bottles for perfume. These had been in her trousseau and she let me play pretend with them.

I had dolls to play with. My favorite was a baby doll with a cloth body, and porcelain head and hands. I carried it around on a cushion, so it wouldn't break. But it did not survive being shared with my siblings. Mostly, I remember small china dolls with stiff legs and arms that moved. I learned to sew doll clothes for them on Mama's treadle sewing machine. I had a small suitcase in which I kept both dolls and their clothes. I also played with paper dolls, spending most of my time making new clothes for them. Paper dolls were printed in women's magazines to be colored and cut out. They were also sold in books. We also made paper dolls from large dress pattern books.

Play is an important part of childhood. It permits children to explore and try out various roles of adulthood without commit-ment or penalty. Pretend is serious practice for future behavior. In retrospect, I realize that in our sandbox my brother and I were exploring the activities and roles of our parents and other adults who influenced our lives. We were very conscious of our gender, but not with any sexual consciousness. It was an imitation of our expectations for our future roles as grownups. I spent much time alone as a child in unstructured activities. My pastimes became games only after I learned to play with others.

For my brother and me, social games came with growth, physical control, and mastery of our language. The value of our sand box play was the freedom to use our own imaginations and to create many of our toys. We spent many happy days in that sand box built in the corner of the ell of our house.

SCHOOL AT LAST

Ding, Dong! Ding, Dong! The bell on top of the school house sounded in every corner of the Fort and this time the school bell was ringing for me! I had been ready for an hour before Mama let me go. Then, with my new lunch box in hand, I ran across the lawn to Aunt Phoebe's house and rapped on the screen door. I was going to walk with Gene, because she had started school the year before and she knew just what to do. It was early September, 1928. I would not be six until my birthday in November, but I had been given special permission to enroll so that I could transfer to the school in Logan when we returned after the farm was closed for the winter.

"Come in," Aunt Phoebe called, "You're early. We'll be ready in a minute." She was brushing Gene's curls around her finger to make ringlets. On any other day I would be envious of those curls, but that morning I felt just fine with my new Dutch cut. I waited impatiently, while Aunt Phoebe gathered Genes curls and tied them back with a new ribbon.

"Now run along," she said as she handed Gene her lunch pail. Aunt Phoebe stood in the doorway and watched as we hurried down the wooden walk and turned into the road where we joined the Seeley children.

"Hi Skinner! So you're goin' to school at last," Grant taunted. He ran ahead to join the boys. Gene and I were joined by his big sister, Helen, and we followed the boys up the row until we came to Crumbo's. Shirley and Rose were waiting for us. Elmer came out of the hotel and ran off with the boys, cutting across the parade ground. We girls scuffed along through yellow leaves, walking around the row.

When we reached the school, we set our lunch pails on the steps and played tag while children from distant parts of the reservation gathered. There was no school bus, but there was a stable and a hitching post out back. Most pupils lived near enough to the Fort to walk to school. A few of the Native American children came from some distance, so they rode ponies which were stabled behind the school.

The school stood in the southwest corner of the Fort and, like all the other buildings, it was painted gray. It had a belfry on top of the building with a large black bell that looked like the Liberty Bell. There was no lawn in the yard, but there was a very large tree. A porch with a metal pipe railing extended across the front of the school. The restrooms were in a lean-to added to the rear of the building.

At nine o'clock the tardy bell rang. We formed two lines, boys in one line and girls in the other. We marched up the steps and into the hallway where we deposited our lunch pails on a shelf over the hooks for coats. The school smelled of chalk and coal oil. A hallway separated the building into two classrooms, the principal's office, and a storeroom. Before entering the classroom, we formed two lines again–first to fourth graders in one line and fifth to eighth graders in the other. Usually, we marched to our desk and stood until our teacher invited us to sit down. Because this was the first day of school, our teacher stood at the door and greeted each of us by name, indicating which desk we should take. I was assigned to Mrs. Jorgensen's room, which was called the Primary Room. Grades five to eight met in the Grammar room with the principal, Mr. Panter, as their teacher.

Each classroom had a wood-burning stove. The teacher's desk was at the rear, and it stood on a raised platform in the corner. The Primary classroom was furnished with rows of various sized desks, the larger ones at the rear, and the smaller ones at the front. I was assigned to a small desk, next to the window. The top of my desk was slanted, and hinged at the top with space to store books and papers inside. There was a hole for an inkwell and a little carved slot for a pencil. We were each given a new cedar pencil, a pair of scissors, a box of crayons and an orange notebook. It said "Golden West" on the cover, and there was a line at the bottom to write my name and grade number.

Readers were piled on shelves beneath the window. They were passed to each pupil as needed. When there were not enough to go around, we squeezed together two to a desk and shared the same book. A slate blackboard covered one wall. A chalk rail hung beneath it. Every few inches along the rail was an eraser hanging from a string. Along the top of the blackboard was a row of the big and little letters of the alphabet. On the far side of the room were wooden chairs of varied size. They were painted different colors. The reading groups were named by colors to match the chairs. Everyone began as a Bluebird, sitting on the smallest blue chairs, and advanced through yellow, green and red chairs.

Pupils began school at six years of age. I would not be six until my birthday in November, but I had already learned to read. Reading began as a game that we played during the long journeys between Logan and Fort Duchesne. Each time we encountered a new road sign, Mama would ask, "What does it spell?" I would sound out the letters and learn a new word. I soon discovered I could read words everywhere by this method. An old family joke developed because I could not understand why the sign WIND-ING ROAD had a different sound than the word *wind*. There were lots of WINDING ROAD signs in the canyons, and I was teased each time we came to one, because I had insisted on pronouncing it to rhyme with wind.

According to the rules, Mr. Panter could not let me enroll before my sixth birthday. But Mama and Aunt Phoebe persuaded him to reconsider, so one day before school started, I went with Mama to his office to prove to him that I could read. I wanted to start school very much.

Mr. Panter sat in a large swivel chair in front of a roll top desk. He had a round belly and wore dark rimmed glasses which hung down on his nose, so he could look over the tops of them. He looked very comical and I wanted to laugh, but his manner was very intimidating so I didn't dare. After asking me some questions, he selected a book from the pile on his desk. Opening it at random, he handed it to me. "Now read to me," he said. Ah, this is easy I thought, I recognized the primer. In fact, I knew the story by heart. *The Ginger Bread Man* was a favorite story of mine. I had read it many times, having found it among the story books in Aunt Phoebe's attic. Leaving the open book lying in my lap, I recited every word. I never once took my eyes off Mr.

Panter's face. He selected another book, and another, until he found a book without any pictures, and with pages filled with all new words. After I read a few lines, he granted me permission to enroll, saying I was to begin reading with the second grade reader. Otherwise, I was a new first grader.

Mrs. Jorgensen was very pretty with curly blonde hair and blue eyes. She spoke softly and smiled a lot. Besides being the Primary teacher, she taught singing to both classrooms. She used a pitch pipe, because there was no piano in the school. I liked her very much, and I liked school. Much of the class work was oral recitation. The teacher took turns with each class. She assigned work to one class, then while we worked on the assignment, she went to the next class. We had to learn to concentrate on our own work, while those next to us were doing something different. But this also made it convenient to listen to the recitation of pupils more advanced than ourselves. I remember rolling ropes of clay on my desk while I listened to the third graders read, thus I became an advanced reader. Older children drilled younger ones, and slower ones. Often it was one of the older pupils who led spelling drills, or listened to us recite our times tables. About the only thing every pupil did all at the same time was sing together, and listen at story time. Mrs. Jorgensen told us a story every Friday afternoon. One that I remember was a Native American story about "Coyote."

This is the story about Coyote:

Coyote was running along, running along. He ran a long way, and grew very tired and very thirsty. At last he came to a small lake, where he stopped for a drink of water. As he leaned over to drink, he looked into the lake. He saw a very big fish. Coyote was very frightened by the fish, so he ran away without drinking. After a little while, Coyote crept back to the water. He was still very thirsty and he really wanted to drink, but he was afraid of the big fish, so he lay down by the water to watch. Soon Antelope came loping along, loping along. Antelope walked right up to the lake and drank a long drink, then went on his way.

Coyote saw that the big fish had not frightened Antelope, so he crept closer to the water and looked in.

This time Antelope saw Frog sitting on the bottom. Coyote asked Frog, "Why did you frighten me?"
"Silly old Coyote! There's nothing in the water" Frog said, laughing. "You were frightened by your own shadow."
So, Coyote shut his eyes and drank a long drink of water. Frog and Coyote had a good laugh. Then Coyote went running along, running along.

The children laughed at Frog and Coyote, too. I laughed again, when I retold the story at supper time. I attended school at Fort Duchesne for only a few weeks. I never heard the school bell ring for me at Fort Duchesne again.

WONG SING

Wong Sing, ca. 1928
Courtesy of L. C. Thorne Collection

The road to Wong Sing's crossed the bridge just outside the entrance to the Fort, then meandered easterly along the base of a jagged red stone mesa, turning past a green field of alfalfa edged by a grove of cottonwoods. There was Wong Sing's! The distance was about a mile. On my sixth birthday, November 28, 1928, I went with my father to Wong Sing's to fetch a surprise. I had waited impatiently for Daddy's working day to end. When at last he came, I climbed up into his farm truck and settled onto the narrow leather seat. Leaning forward, I wished speed into the turning wheels that left plumes of red sand behind us.

The day was sunny, but the air was crisp and cool. Indian Summer had spread a special glow on the now leafless trees. We rattled over the long rusty bridge which stretched like a giant tinker toy over a river of stones. The stones were self-arranged in the dry river bottom, and formed a giant mosaic paving to mark the water course. No water moved over the round stones, nor was there any evidence of the violence of the spring torrents which tumbled them along their journey from the high Uinta's.

Wong Sing's trading post consisted of half a dozen low wooden buildings lined up along the roadside. They were tied together by a plank porch and a hitching rail that marked the edge of the road. Over the door to the biggest building hung a sign which read:

WONG SING GENERAL MERCHANDISE.

An irrigation ditch along one side of the buildings impounded a small reservoir which served as a watering trough for horses. A narrow bridge and footpath led to a clump of trees, sheltering a tiny house built of river stones where Wong Sing lived. Cars, horse drawn wagons and booted cowboys, all stopped at the rail.

Daddy, too, stopped at the hitching rail. I jumped down and ran toward the main door. Usually open, on that day it was closed against the cold November air. As I pushed open the door, a waft of exotic smells poured out. The draft set into motion a colorful glass wind chime which hung over the counter, sending a delightful cascade of notes to summon Wong Sing from his storeroom.

When I knew Wong Sing, he had been in business more than forty years. His round face was ageless and smiling. As I entered, he came toward me. Grinning, he bowed slightly, "Ah! Missy Blue Eyes, yoh have come foh yoh plize? Come, fust we toast yoh buthday." With a fat finger he beckoned me to follow him.

I followed Wong Sing down a narrow aisle between tea boxes, chests and lumpy sacks which were stacked from floor to ceiling. His moccasin shod feet moved silently over the worn board floor. He wore a black silk cap and he was dressed like the Indians in beaded moccasins, jeans, silk shirt and vest. He smoked cigars and smelled of aromatic tobacco. Sunshine poured through the open door at the far end of the storeroom. There, Wong Sing stopped beside a huge oak cask. With great ceremony, he picked up a large green glass and held it under the wooden spigot. An amber stream of apple cider poured into the glass. Filling my glass to the brim, and another one for himself, he raised his glass, "Yoh big gull now. We dlink!"

I thanked him, and emptied the glass. With a round gentle hand he smoothed my white hair and handed me a narrow red silk box embroidered with golden flowers. Inside lay a string of blue glass beads. Holding them up to the sunlight, they flashed prisms of color into the shadows. Sliding them over my head Wong Sing said, "To smile, like yoh eyes foh me. Happy Buthday!"

And so, smiling like a recently crowned princess, I returned to the salesroom where a fire burned in a potbellied stove flanked by the benches that sat on the porch in summertime. On one of them sat a large box tied with red ribbon.

"Foh Happiness!" Wong Sing exclaimed, as he helped me cut the ribbon. Inside was a child-sized rocking chair, which I had wished for all summer. It was just like the one in our cozy book-lined reading room–golden oak with a square back and arms. Now that I had started school, I would have my very own reading chair. Wong Sing set the chair beside the stove and I sat down in it to wait for Daddy, who had business to discuss with Wong Sing.

I looked around as I rocked in my new chair. Near the door Wong Wing sat on a high stool inside a bamboo-like cage, alternately clicking beads on his abacus, and painting characters on long slips of paper with a brush dipped in ink. Unlike his father, Wing was tall and slim, and he wore a white shirt with the sleeves rolled up. His face was very round, and his dark eyes sparkled when he smiled. He was speaking Ute to two men who filled flour sacks with their purchases. Wing stopped counting and winked at me as he lifted the top from a glass jar filled with colorful lollipops, indicating I should help myself. " 'Tis your birthday today Missy? Be happy today, and always."

"Thank you," I said and chose an orange lollipop.

I sat down in my little chair, licked the lollipop and looked around. The store was a virtual bazaar. It contained everything imaginable. Just inside the door the bookkeeping area where Wing worked was partitioned off with bamboo. Behind the meat counter, where sawdust covered the floor, an old Chinese, called Wee, presided over the butcher shop. In the grocery department sacks of flour and sugar were stacked in rows. Piled on the counter were wheels of cheese, tins of crackers, and colored candy in glass jars. Huge, burlap sacks of grain and seeds stood open along one wall. A large scale hung from the ceiling over bins filled with nails and hardware supplies. Shoes and boots hung from a line overhead. Bolts of silk and cotton spilled over a large table.

Wooden drawers contained dried herbs and medicines. Bars of soap, tins of spices, and exotic glass jars filled the shelves, adding to the potpourri of scents. Inside a glass case, strings of pearls, glass beads, perfumes, folding ivory fans, coloring books, crayons, and paper dolls crowded the shelves. Furniture and farm equipment filled adjoining buildings. Hanging from large pegs were horse collars and harness, saddles and wagon wheels. Indian rugs, blankets, and shawls were piled between wooden chairs and iron bedsteads. And on the walls hung Indian drums, spears, baskets, beaded saddle blankets, leggings, gloves, and other artifacts taken in trade for food and tobacco. Wong Sing's was a warehouse of enchantment.

Going to Wong Sing's at any time was a special kind of adventure. It was the only store near the Agency. During summer, we often made the journey on the footpath crossing through the river bottom. In summer, it was a delight for then only small pools of green water remained of the river. The trail began below the pump house, crossed over hot rocks and sand bars, and then threaded its way under a canopy of green leaves. The gray limbs of the cottonwoods stretched skyward, resembling the stone ribs of a Gothic cathedral. Dust motes danced in the sun beams glinting through the leaves. The trail emerged finally onto an alfalfa field across the road from Wong Sing's store. We crossed it along the irrigation ditch that drained into the river.

Next to the ragtag collection of buildings stood a clump of trees growing on a patchy lawn, which also served as a picnic and playground for the women and children, who waited outside while the men did their trading and visiting in the store. For his customer's convenience, Wong Sing provided a large wooden picnic table, and a standpipe of clean drinking water.

Sometimes we were sent to Wong Sing's to buy something as simple as a spool of thread or a bottle of vanilla extract. More often we had a list of things that would be delivered to the Fort the next day in Wong Sing's delivery wagon.

As a child, it did not seem strange to me that the trading post on the Indian reservation should be run by the only Chinese I ever knew. Long after I left Fort Duchesne, I became curious about Wong Sing. I wondered how he came to live among the

Indians. What I learned about Wong Sing was as romantic as anything I remembered.

Wong Sing had not always been round and jolly. In the beginning his boyish figure was dressed in the conventional padded blue cotton clothes of the Chinese laborer and he wore the long queue decreed by the Manchu Emperor as a sign of servitude. He was born in Canton, and was recruited by the Six Companies to labor in the gold mines in California. Like most Chinese sojourners, Wong Sing left his home in China confident that he would return from America as a wealthy and honorable merchant. Wong Sing's trading post became legendary, but it had begun humbly.

On a bend in the river just below Fort Duchesne, young Wong Sing established what was the only Chinese laundry ever located on the Ute Reservation. The year was 1889, a mere two years after the army post at Fort Duchesne was established. There, in the unlikely desert of sage brush and sand, populated mostly with Indians, the young Cantonese immigrant found his *Gum Shan*, or Gold Mountain, among the Utes of eastern Utah.

Wong Sing made his way to Fort Duchesne by way of San Francisco and the silver mines. In 1889, there were two troops of cavalry, and a company of infantry stationed at the Fort. After an unsuccessful attempt to establish a restaurant at Ouray, Wong Sing built a primitive laundry on the banks of the Uinta River near the entrance gate of the stockaded Fort. Bending over washtubs filled with water taken from the river and heated on open fires of driftwood, Wong Sing washed clothes for the soldiers stationed at the Fort. He spread the clothes to dry on the wild rose bushes and willows growing on the river banks. His laundry prospered, and Wong Sing expanded his services. He acquired pieces of chinaware, ribbons and trinkets which he sold to the officer's wives when he delivered their laundry. Thus began his career in merchandising.

While working in his laundry, Wong Sing came into contact with the Utes. He mastered several dialects of their language, but his speaking ability in English remained limited. Wong Sing's first big opportunity came when an enterprising pair of troopers opened a poker game in a rented room at the Fort Duchesne Hotel. Wong Sing was a skillful gambler, and his Chinese face was inscrutable. He played with both soldiers and Indians. With his winnings, together with the profits from his laundry and china sales, he started a small restaurant and a little store on the grounds of the Fort.

His successful dealings with the Indians aroused jealousy on the part of several white settlers who plotted to have his store banished from government property. Determined to continue his commercial activities, Wong Sing purchased a few acres of land across the river about a mile and a half east of the Fort, on what was known as *The Strip*. The Strip was an area of some 7,000 acres in the western part of Uintah County, adjoining Fort Duchesne along its eastern boundary. It had been segregated from the Uintah Reservation by Act of Congress because of the presence of a vein of asphalt, or Gilsonite (uintaite), for which northeastern Utah was famous in those years.

The Strip soon gained notoriety for violence. A log saloon was located there, and outside the boundary of the military post. It became known as a den for gamblers, prostitutes, intoxicated soldiers, and the local inhabitants. Arguments generated in the saloon resulted in several violent incidents. Beyond direct jurisdiction of either the Agency or the Army, *The Strip* became a sort of no-man's land where only the nonresident sheriff had power to enforce the county's law. After much pressure to abolish this den of iniquity, the Uintah County Commissioners terminated the license for the saloon. The commanding officer at the Fort placed vigorous restrictions on the troops. A guard was posted on the bridge over the Uinta River to search all vehicles crossing it. The outlaw ways in *The Strip* were suppressed.

This was Wong Sing's opportunity. He purchased the abandoned saloon, and moved it to his land as the first of the string of buildings which became his trading post. As his reputation grew and his business prospered, his range of acquaintances widened. Wong Sing cut his queue, and adopted the moccasin of the Indian. He shipped goods far beyond the limits of eastern Utah and the Reservation. Each year he distributed colorful calendars which depicted the culture of the Indians.

As his growing business required additional space, he acquired other old buildings which were added to his original store. There were three or four frame houses with mismatched roofs standing side by side. They were a ragtag assemblage of abandoned frontier buildings which Wong Sing found useful, and which all his customers enjoyed.

Wong Sing's Trading Post
Courtesy of Norma Denver

In 1928, Wong Sing employed eight clerks. When the Depression set in, he reduced his force and extended credit to his trusted customers. He had a reputation for scrupulous honesty. His personal checks were honored as cash by all the banks in Salt Lake City, and were accepted by the U.S. Post Office. In fact, he frequently cashed government vouchers so that the large sums of cash needed for payment of the Indian allotments did not have to be transported over the isolated road between Salt Lake City and the Agency.

Wong Sing's loyal customers delighted in the often repeated story of the salesman who tried to sell him an adding machine to replace his abacus. Wong Sing saw no advantage in the new machine, but he accepted the salesman's challenge to a race adding up a long column of figures. Not only did Wong Sing finish first, but when their totals differed Wong Sing's proved to be correct. The salesman had pushed a wrong key on his machine.

On March 21, 1934, Wong Sing was returning to Fort Duchesne from Salt Lake City. Near Snyderville, his truck was forced off the road by a passing car. His truck overturned, and Wong Sing died instantly. The people in the Uintah Basin were stunned by his untimely death. Wong Sing had been more than a successful businessman. His friends, Indians and Whites alike, deeply mourned his death. At Fort Duchesne, sixty Indian braves met in a solemn tribal council to extol his virtues, and mourn his passing.

Not all of Wong Sing's efforts were devoted to business. He quietly conducted welfare work among the Indians, assisting them in their business transactions. He preserved many of their fine artifacts. He photographed many of their tribal customs and ceremonies. He was generous in the White community with his support of the scientific and commercial development of the Basin. His benefactions had been many and generous. His loss was deeply felt.

Wong Sing had returned to China as a wealthy and successful merchant, but he did not stay in Canton. He brought his son, Wong Wing, back to share in the bounty of his adopted land. After Wong Sing's death, Wing moved the buildings once more. Facing the improved highway, U.S. 40, they bore a new name: WONG C. WING, MERC. Wing continued the mercantile business until it was again sold.

When the Utes built the Bottle Hollow Resort on the site of the old rodeo grounds, a merchant named Brotherson opened a country store, and used the old buildings as warehouses. Behind the country store stood the old picnic table, now covered with the carved initials and names of Wong Sing's customers and friends. Like a large rune stone, the table recorded the deeds of a local hero.

Wong Sing served his neighbors and friends with integrity. He contributed greatly to a better understanding between the races living on, and near, the Reservation. Due to the wide distribution of his calendars, he was known throughout the West. He was rewarded with material success, and the same measure of devotion which he extended to those he served. Wong Sing died an Honorable Merchant, and an Honorary member of the Ute tribe. He will never be forgotten by those who knew him, most especially his little friends who were always received with his friendly smile and a jar filled with free lollipops, as he queried, "Yoh velly good today?"

GAMES
AND
PASTIMES

Across the lawn is The Children's Home

THE CHILDREN'S HOME

One afternoon Aunt Phoebe was sitting in her rocking chair, reading from the book which rested in her lap. Gene and I were playing with paper dolls spread out upon the oilcloth which covered the kitchen table.

"It's mine," declared Gene, reaching for my favorite Dolly Dingle.

"No! It's mine!" I insisted, holding on as Gene's fingers closed around the head and separated it from the body.

"Now look what you've done," I protested, trying to fit the pieces together.

"Time for a picnic!" Aunt Phoebe announced, putting aside her book. She removed her spectacles, folded them, and slipped them into her apron pocket as she stood up. She began to gather up the paper dolls and laid them in a candy box. "A bit of paste and it will be good as new," she comforted. Playing games was her way of disciplining children, and she suggested one whenever trouble arose.

"I think a pretend picnic would be nice," she said. "Where would you like to go?" Aunt Phoebe loved picnics, especially if they were impromptu.

"Can we go to the Gypsy Camp?" we asked in one voice.

"Can Mae go too?" Gene asked.

"And Leroy?" I added.

"There's room for everyone," answered Aunt Phoebe. Her blue eyes twinkled with excitement, as the pretense began. Pretending all the while, we found a large basket and set it on the table. We made pretend sandwiches and loaded all the good things we liked, naming them as we filled the basket. We laughed and argued as to whether we would have chocolate cake, or oatmeal cookies.

"We shall have both," Aunt Phoebe laughed, "now run and ask your mother, then gather your friends. We'll leave in ten minutes," she said, taking off her apron.

Minutes later a ragtag group of children gathered beside Aunt Phoebe's garden gate. Leroy and Garth wore blue and white striped overalls and high-topped shoes. Halley wore overalls too, but he was wearing moccasins without socks. His brown back was bare and his black hair was topped by a multicolored beanie studded with bottle caps. Mae, Gene and I were wearing cotton dresses that covered our boney knees, and we wore sturdy leather-soled shoes and ankle socks. Everyone else wore straw hats, but I wore a sun bonnet that matched my dress. Aunt Phoebe tied on her straw garden hat with a long blue ribbon and asked, "Everyone here? Now you must stay together," she cautioned, handing Gene the pretend picnic basket to carry. "Now, don't drop it," she said, reaching over, and lifting the latch of the wooden gate.

We crossed the vegetable garden in single file, being careful to walk in the irrigation furrows. We climbed over the fence and crossed the dirt road. We circled around the stable and headed down the sandy trail past the barns and corrals, past the pump house and watering trough, to the edge of the river. Only pools of shallow water remained among the round river stones that formed the broad bottom of the Uinta River.

The Gypsy Camp was a wide sandy beach in the bend of the river. It was shaded by cottonwood trees, and clumps of huckleberries and willows. The sand sloped down to a deep pool that served as our swimming hole. It was located less than a quarter of a mile upstream from Fort Duchesne. Aunt Phoebe had named it the Gypsy Camp when she first came to live at the Fort, because it also served as a campground for Native Americans who came to the Fort from other parts of the reservation on business of various kinds.

From the Gypsy Camp, we walked along the pebbled water course, stepping from one sand island to another. The river stones were striped due to the variously colored shales and layers of mud that had formed the mountains from which the river flowed, tumbling the rocks so that they were round and smooth. The river bottom smelled of nettles and resinous weeds. Wedged against the banks, or stranded in the rocks, were uprooted trees and jumbled piles of driftwood baking in the sun. Lizards scurried into the rocks, and birds took flight as we made our noisy way along, stepping gingerly from island to island of sand.

Coming to an island completely surrounded by shallow water, Aunt Phoebe stepped gaily across the narrow stream and plopped down onto the sand. "Aha! It's the perfect island for our picnic! Let's pretend we're marooned," she said.

Barely room for all of us, we crowded onto the little island. Aunt Phoebe pretended to take the basket and set it on the sand. She shook out the cloth, and spread it on the sand. Then, still pretending, she solemnly handed each of us a make-believe sandwich. Filling cups with make-believe lemonade, she passed one to each of us. We pretended to eat, wishing that at least the lemonade were real. Extending her empty hand to Leroy, he burst into disappointed tears and cried, "But I don't see anything!"

"Why, of course not," Aunt Phoebe replied. "This is a pretend picnic! You have no imagination whatsoever. It's time to go home and have lunch."

The picnic was over. We raced back to the pump house where a large pipe overflowed into an old bath tub used as a watering trough for horses. The water was tinged yellow with chlorine, but it was safe for children to drink. Taking turns, we bent over the pipe and drank from cupped hands. Thus ended one of Aunt Phoebe's typical games.

Aunt Phoebe's front hall was a fascinating place. Mounted on the long wall were several telephones of various vintage and design. There were no private residential telephone lines at the Fort, so all calls had to be placed to the operators in Roosevelt or Vernal from Aunt Phoebe's front hall. There was a separate long distance phone for Salt Lake City which was used for emergencies.

My favorite telephone was a long oak box with a protruding mouthpiece that curved downward. I stood on my tip toes so I could talk into it. A heavy bell-shaped ear piece was suspended from a hook on one side of the box. A large silver crank extended from the other side. Turning the crank, rang the operator who demanded, "Number please! What number are you calling?" After you told her the number, she plugged your line into the switchboard that connected you to the telephone of the person you were calling. You could hear it ring, then the person would answer. It was like magic to talk to someone in a different town.

Since telephone conversations were rare and expensive, they were usually limited to important business. I always arrived at Aunt Phoebe's hopeful that I would be dispatched as a messenger to summon someone at the Fort to the telephone.

Behind Aunt Phoebe's dining room door was a teletype machine that printed words on paper tape. These words were cut and pasted on the yellow telegram sheets, then folded and put into envelopes. Any child might be pressed into service as a messenger, but only Aunt Phoebe was allowed to receive the messages, for their contents were considered to be private information. Occasionally, I would be allowed to deliver the telegram sealed in a bright yellow envelope. Though it made us feel very important to run down the row waving our yellow envelope, I am sure Aunt Phoebe never sent us off with bad news. We were delighted with the nickel we received for delivering the telegram.

Aunt Phoebe had another magic machine in her parlor. Standing against one wall was an automatic pianola. It looked like any ordinary piano, but hers had sliding doors behind the music rack that opened to reveal the automatic brass rollers. In front of the key board was a drawer that pulled open. In it were levers that controlled the rollers. Pumping foot pedals activated the rollers and a bellows that blew air through perforations in the paper wound around the rollers, causing the piano to play music all by itself. The machinery depressed the proper piano keys to play different tunes, as if a phantom with unseen hands were playing the keys.

I can see us still. Gene had longer legs than I, so she could pump faster than I could. I usually ended up pumping the left pedal with both feet, while Gene pumped the right one.
If the music was a little lopsided, it didn't matter. We rummaged through the stacked boxes of music rolls. Taking a roll from the box, Gene slid open the little door behind the music rack, and set the roller in the bracket. Then, like a window shade, she pulled a length of perforated paper and threaded it over the empty brass roller with little holes in it. She tucked the end into a slot and adjusted the levers. "Now pump!" she commanded. We pumped, and sang, giggling while we tried to sing. It was glorious fun and permitted even a novice to play without piano lessons.

John Pappas was a frequent visitor to the Children's Home.

He was a Greek sheepherder, who lived near the intersection of the highway and the road turning into the Fort. He usually wore a wild and wooly fleece jacket just like his unshorn sheep. He smelled of tobacco and garlic. I shrank from his demand for "Kisses, kisses!" But no child can resist genuine affection, and I could not deny his flashing black eyes.

"Come on girlie, let's dance," he cried, sweeping me up with a great bear hug and twirling me around in a circle, his wild black mustache flying. The dishes rattled as his booted feet skipped across Aunt Phoebe's kitchen floor.

Gene's sister, Mae, was an expert candy maker. When she came to visit, we coaxed her to make honey candy. She got out the big heavy candy kettle, and we stoked up the fire. She poured honey into the kettle from a huge square ten-gallon can. She never had to measure the honey. Taking a huge wooden spoon, and guiding my hand she said, "Keep stirring so the bottom doesn't scorch. Like this!" She made big figure eights in the melting honey. When the honey began to boil, Mae took the spoon, because she didn't want us to be burned. We watched it foam up to the brim of the pot, as Mae stirred faster and faster. Gradually, the candy sank into a smooth bubbly mass. "Time to test it," said Mae, lifting the spoon and counting the drops that dripped off the edge of the spoon into a cup of cold water. She worked the glob of candy into a ball with her fingers, and cracked it on the edge of the cup. "Perfect!" she said, pulling the heavy pot to the back of the stove. She poured the hot candy into a large flat pan which we had coated with butter. When it was cool enough to handle, Mae divided it into lumps. She gave each of us a handful to pull. As we stretched it, the candy was transformed. The amber lumps became skeins of gold. We stretched and stretched it, pulling it into long skinny ropes which were laid onto buttered brown paper to harden. While it was still warm, Mae broke it into bite-size pieces which we popped into our mouths. "Mmm, delicious!" nothing better than Uintah Basin honey, unless it was made into honey candy.

One thing that Aunt Phoebe heartily frowned upon was someone sitting on her kitchen table. Since it stood in the middle of the room it was very tempting to lean on, or sit on and often there were more children than chairs. Gene's big brother, Harold, who loved to play practical jokes, decided to teach us all a lesson. One evening, we were seated around the table playing Parcheesi. A couple of extra people came to use the telephone. Our game was interrupted temporarily when we got up to offer our chairs to the guests. When no one was looking, Harold connected the wire he had concealed beneath the oilcloth to batteries that were behind the door. Without thinking, Grant swung up to perch on the edge of the table.

"Yeow!" he yelled, leaping off the hot seat. Harold and Bill collapsed in paroxysms of laughter. Aunt Phoebe smiled knowingly from her rocking chair. "Well, I guess that will teach you not to sit on my table." It did all right.

Gene's brother, Bill, loved to sing. For years I believed that his plaintive ballads about *Little Dogies, Laredo,* and *The Big Rock Candy Mountain* had been composed just for me. I loved his songs and his guitar, but Bill was also a terrible tease who became a pest when he interfered with the girlish games of dolls, dress-up, and Trinkets that Gene and I played.

My favorite brother was dark-haired Bob. Like his mother, Phoebe, he was gregarious, playful, and always ready to help. He did not tease, and he could always be relied upon to fix things. He was the favorite captain for our games of "Run Sheep, Runnn." Sometimes his imagination ran away with him, like the time he wired the garden hose into an old inner tube. He wanted to see how big it would get. For two whole days we watched it swell, growing bigger and bigger as it slowly filled with water. It looked like a giant red sausage that we expected to burst open and spout up like a geyser. But that didn't happen. It split along the bottom and the water just oozed out quietly, flooding the lawn when no one was watching.

At the Children's Home, there were new puppies and kittens to cuddle. Because we moved twice each year, we were not permitted to have a dog of our own. The only pets Leroy and I knew and loved belonged there. Faithful and unforgettable was Homer. Homer had been a working sheep dog. Now grown old, his long gray hair hung down and covered his eyes. I could never understand how he could see where he was going. He followed us everywhere. His favorite game was retrieving sticks that we threw for him.

Aunt Phoebe taught us how to make dancing ladies from hollyhock blossoms. By the dozen, we sent our pink and crimson-gowned ladies swirling across the grass to the imagined strains of a waltz.

I remember little tin buckets spilling over with black currants, gooseberries, and wild chokecherries that we gathered when Aunt Phoebe took us berry picking in the river bottom. She showed us how to gather the soft down from milk weed that grew along the irrigation ditches. We spread it out to dry in the sun, and then used it to stuff doll quilts and pillows. She showed us how to make chewing gum by breaking milkweed stems and collecting the milky sap. With our thumbs we rolled the sap into a wad in the palm of our hand, and then stuffed it into our mouths. It tasted kind of bitter, but it was more readily available than the bubble gum we bought at Wong Sing's store.

Aunt Phoebe went with us to hunt for feathers and robins' eggs. She showed us where to look for fossils and wild flowers. We pulled petals from her daisies in order to discover "who loves me loves me not." We searched in her grass for a lucky four-leaf clover. And we played mumbletypeg with the boys in the shade of her porch. After supper we gathered on the lawn beside the Children's Home, watching for the first star of the evening to make a wish upon. We waited for fireflies and hid from bats that darted across the evening sky, fearful that if we stood still, they might build nests in our hair. Aunt Phoebe named the constellations, telling their stories as they appeared. We became familiar with the big and the little Dipper, the Pleiades, Orion, and the North Star. With no ground lights to diminish their brightness the stars of the Milky Way swept across the sky like a bright pathway, inviting us to follow where it led.

When the crickets sang, we found places on Aunt Phoebe's front steps for storytelling. She was a wonderful storyteller, and she never ran out of stories. Many of them were about her own experiences. Some she had read, some were Indian tales, some were stories about the pioneers who had crossed the plains, and settled in the valley. She encouraged us to tell our stories, too. It was a nice quiet time, sitting there on the wooden steps in the long shadows of the tall trees.

"Tell us a story," we begged. Aunt Phoebe sat down on the steps, and wrapped her arms around her knees as we all crowded close to make room.

"You promised us a ghost story," said Garth.

"Do you believe there are ghosts at sea?" she asked softly,

Once upon a time a ship was sailing from Scotland. The wind began to blow, and it was caught in a great storm. The wind blew harder, and harder, and the waves rose higher, and higher. Finally, the Mate ordered some of his boys up into the rigging, to reef the topsails. Up the mast, and into the wind they climbed. The first sailor started up the shrouds, and when he reached the yardarm, he heard a strange voice saying, "It blows hard!"

The lad waited no more. He scrambled down in a twinkling and told the others what he had heard. "There's a strange voice up there, shouting a warning!"

"Scaredy cat," a second sailor scoffed, and climbed up the mast. But he descended even more quickly than the first. "It be a ghost, cryin' loud, It blows hard!"

The wind grew stronger, and the ship heeled wildly. The Mate sent another sailor went up to the yard arm. Then another, and another, but each came back with the same tale. At length the Mate, having sent up the whole watch, ran up the shrouds himself. When he reached the haunted spot, he heard the dreadful words uttered in his ear. "It blows hard!"

"Aye, aye, old one. But blow it ever so hard, we must ease the tops'l for all that," shouted the Mate. Reaching for the line, he saw a parrot perched on one of the yardarms. So, that was the author of the false alarms! He caught the bird and carried it down to the deck.

"There's yer ghost," he said.

Aunt Phoebe finished her tale. We laughed, and clamored for another story, but Aunt Phoebe quietly said, "It's curfew time. It's been a busy day. There will be other days." Standing up, she said, "Good night all."

And, there were. So many happy days were spent at The Children's Home!

CELEBRATIONS IN JULY

In Utah, July is a month of celebrations. First, comes the traditional Independence Day on July 4th. Pioneer Day, on July 24th, commemorates the arrival of Brigham Young and the first company of Mormon pioneers into the Salt Lake Valley in 1847. In the Uinta Basin, observance of these days rotated between Roosevelt and Vernal. In the days between, many Mormon families held their family reunions. All these celebrations had several things in common--a parade, a community picnic, fireworks, root beer, and homemade ice cream.

About the middle of June, we began to get ready for the Fourth of July Celebration. Traditionally, my family contributed homemade root beer. Making it required several days to ferment slowly. It also required many hands and lots of space. Mama organized the work, which included all the children at the Fort. We set up on our back lawn, so that spilled water and syrup could be washed away with the garden hose. We made a long table by laying planks across saw horses.

We began the root beer making by washing the green and brown bottles that had been stored all winter. When the bottles were clean, Mama scalded them with boiling water. Then we were ready to make the root beer. We mixed it in a large white enamel pan, which had also served as a baby bath tub. We measured several pounds of sugar into the pan. We poured the root beer extract over the sugar, and added several gallons of hot water to dissolve the sugar. We stirred the concentrated syrup until the sugar was completely dissolved, and then we added more water to dilute it. Dissolved yeast was added to the mixture which then had to be stirred again until it was mixed thoroughly.

After the sugar, water, and yeast had been properly mixed we were ready to begin filling the bottles. We formed a regular production line for this step. The dipper filled a large enamel pitcher, and passed it on to the filler. The filler placed a funnel into a quart-sized bottle, and carefully filled the bottle, leaving about two inches for the fermenting root beer to expand without exploding the bottles. As each bottle was filled, it was passed to the cappers. The first capper applied a cork-lined brass cap to each bottle, then passed it to the second capper. He fitted it under a capper, which clamped the lid onto the bottle by crimping it to form a vacuum seal when the handle was depressed. This operation required sufficient strength and skill to secure the cap without breaking the bottle, or spilling the syrup. The wiper cleaned the filled bottles, and packed them into the clothes basket used to transfer the bottles to our cool dirt cellar where the fermentation occurred. The bottles were laid on their sides between layers of straw. Fermentation occurred slowly, requiring several days. The length of time depended on the weather. If all went well, the root beer would have just the right "bite" in time for the Fourth of July Picnic.

Bottles of root beer were wrapped in blankets, and transported to the picnic in the laundry basket. At the picnic, they were transferred to a large wash tub filled with chunks of ice. By the time the parade was over, the root beer was the proper temperature for drinking. My father ceremoniously opened the bottles, and after tasting it, poured it into tall soda glasses. That root beer warranted its reputation, for it was sheer ambrosia!

Making ice cream was a weekly occurrence at our house. The primary ingredients were a rich cream custard, ice, salt, and shared labor. The ice came from the ice house, and had to be ordered in advance. Ice blocks were packed in cedar sawdust, and stored in the pump house. The sawdust insulated the ice, and kept it frozen all summer. Originally, ice was cut from the frozen river, but in our time it was made of purified water and frozen in an ice plant in Vernal, and then transferred to Fort Duchesne where it was stored.

There were no electric refrigerators at the Fort. Every Saturday morning, the iceman delivered blocks of ice to each household. The horse-drawn ice wagon moved slowly up the alley, stopping at each back door. Children crowded around the dripping wagon, begging for chips and slivers of ice. The iceman wore a large black rubber apron and a shoulder pad. He grasped the ice blocks with big semicircular tongs. Swinging the heavy block up onto his shoulder, he carried it into the kitchen and put it in the ice box. The ice box had a drip pan underneath that had to be emptied every day.

At our house, we always bought an extra chunk of ice for our ice cream freezer. The block of ice was wrapped in a rag rug and stored in a wash tub, until after Sunday School. Our Guernsey cow produced rich milk with thick golden cream. The cow was milked each morning and evening. My father carried it home in a pail, then Mama poured it into flat pans. When the cream floated to the top, it was skimmed off and saved in a bowl to make ice cream and butter. Nothing resembles homemade ice cream made from genuine cream. We did not have thirty flavors. We had vanilla, chocolate, strawberry, and maple nut. Whatever the flavor it was delicious, and left a waxy coating on the roof of your mouth. Mama made her own ice cream cones too. She baked flat thin cookies that were rolled into a cone while still warm from the oven. After they cooled, they were stored in the pantry until needed. They too, were delicious beyond comparison. Ice cream was a real treat. We never tired of it.

After Sunday School, we made ice cream. The freezer was an oak barrel, in which a metal can filled with custard was packed in ice. The can was fitted with paddles attached to a geared top that we turned with a crank. The paddles stirred the custard as the fat molecules in the cream hardened and froze. Stirring while freezing, kept the ice crystals from forming as the custard froze. The can was packed in the barrel with chunks of ice. It was hard work to turn the crank as the creamy custard became solid. Leroy and I took turns, alternately sitting on the freezer to hold it steady, while the other one turned the crank. As the heat from the custard melted the ice, the cold made the custard solid, and it became ice cream. It was a sort of magic process, and the richer the cream was, the better the quality of the ice cream.

When the ice cream became a solid mass so that the crank could no longer be turned, the cover was removed. This was a critical moment, for the canister now floated in a salty slush. Removing the lid, had to be done very carefully so as not to contaminate the ice cream with the salty liquid. After the canister was removed from the barrel, we were allowed to lick the ice cream off the paddles. Unless the ice cream was served immediately, it was packed in fresh ice to keep it frozen. If eaten immediately, it was served in cones or dishes, depending on the occasion. I believe my favorite flavor was maple nut, unless there were fresh strawberries or raspberries to serve over vanilla ice cream.

The Chevy

Our July celebrations always took us away from Fort Duchesne. We went to Roosevelt, Vernal, or the mountains. In any case, the root beer and a barrel of ice cream always went with us. We also took a lavish picnic. While Mama packed lunch, Leroy and I helped wash and polish the car. On patriotic holidays, my father installed a special radiator cap from which fluttered a little bouquet of American flags. We armed ourselves with shiny new cap guns, rolls of caps, and small fire crackers. We had saved our money for weeks, and bought the supplies from Wong Sing's.

The picnic food and ice cream barrel were packed in the trunk. Leroy and I shared the back seat with the basket of root beer. Lorraine sat on Mama's lap, and we were off in time for the ten o'clock parade.

In Vernal, the celebration was always held in the park. The community picnic was spread out on long tables decorated with crepe paper and bunting. We reserved a place in the shade by spreading our cloth and setting the picnic basket on the table.

Then we hastened off to find a place on the curb on Main Street for the parade. The parade included bands, floats, prize horses, clowns, and mounted Native Americans regally dressed in beads and feathers. When it was over, the entire crowd young and old, took their places at the long picnic tables.

Lunch began with a blessing of the food that sometimes seemed more like an oration than a blessing. Then the feast began. Picnic lunches were generously shared. There were huge platters of fried chicken and bowls of potato salad. Other goodies were passed around. Almost no one ate the same food they had brought, for the point was to share, and no one went home hungry. The root beer was shared too. Bottles were passed around, and the root beer was poured into paper cups. The climax was the ice cream served with huge hunks cut from a dozen or more kinds of cakes. All the food was shared, and served up lavishly with friendship and goodwill. Oh, those were great celebrations!

In the park a special platform had been built and draped with bunting. After lunch, the crowd assembled on benches and folding chairs for the Independence Day Oration. The festivities began with the "Pledge of Allegiance" and the singing of *The Star-Spangled Banner*. These were reserved for patriotic events then, not sung at the beginning of every ball game, so that they never became trite. They were performed with reverence and enthusiasm, preparing for the rousing patriotic oration that followed. It went on and on, until finally the end came. The speaker was cheered loudly and the program was brought to an end with the singing of *America The Beautiful*.

While parents rearranged the folding chairs for an afternoon of gossip and politics, the children ran off for the relay races. There were games and contests of skill for all ages. In the park stood a full-sized dinosaur made of cement. It was bombarded with firecrackers all day long. Beyond it was a large lawn where the races were held. Leroy and I raced in a three-legged sack race. We raced to the finish line with each of us tying one foot in a shared gunny sack. We carried peanuts in a spoon in another relay. Then we blew balloons until they burst, threw darts, and tried to hit the clown's face. Prizes were shiny new buffalo nickels which bought a ride on the Merry-Go-Round. There was plenty fun for everyone.

In the evening, a local dance band played for social dancing on an improvised plank floor, under a tent made of strings of colored lights. People of all ages danced into the night while sleepy children were sent home to bed, or fell asleep on the grass.

Roosevelt Parade

When the celebration was held in Roosevelt, the festivities concluded with a fireworks display instead of a dance. The show was staged by Homer P. Edwards, whose house was situated on a high bluff so the fireworks were visible to the whole town. A chute for launching sky rockets pointed out over a steep barren hillside. Mr. Edwards took great pride in his firework display. It began with sparklers for the younger children, and Roman Candles for the older ones. When it was quite dark, the rockets were launched. They shrieked skyward in their wooden track, hissing and exploding into red, green, gold, and silver showers of light.

After all the excitement we rode back to Fort Duchesne. We fell asleep in the back seat, and awoke only when the car crossed the cattle guard at Fort Duchesne. We gathered our loot from the day's festivities, and stumbled sleepily to bed satiated and believing this July Fourth was the best one ever.

Uinta Canyon
Rainie, Virginia, Leroy

GRANDMA ROSE DANIELS

Grandma Rose Daniels

Gene and I were taking turns pushing each other in the big swing that had a wooden seat wide enough for both of to sit on. The swing was hung from a high branch of a tree in the children's playground. Elmer, Halley and Leroy were waxing the wooden slide with bread wrappers. From the top of the slide Elmer yelled, "There she is. She's coming through the gate."

Grandma Rose Daniels was a very old woman, nearly a hundred years old, and she looked it. Her face was deeply creased, and her toothless mouth was drawn in. She stood only about five feet tall, because she was stooped with age. About once a week, she came to spend a day with her daughter, Mentora, who worked at the hotel. She rode into the Fort alone, mounted on her great grey stallion, and seated on a beaded blanket instead of a saddle. She wore a sun bonnet, and a long full skirt tucked into her knee-high moccasins. She held the reins loosely in her gloved hands. Her gloves had huge beaded gauntlets, and she wore several strings of beads that hung down over her long-sleeved blouse. In her saddle bags, she carried flowers and vegetables from her garden. She greeted everyone she passed with a nod or a wave. Everyone at the Fort was her friend.

When she saw us, Grandma's wrinkled face broke into a grin. We raced toward the hitching post by the hotel, each hoping to be the first to greet Grandma Daniels. Only Elmer was her grandson, but everyone called her Grandma, and we loved her for she had been a grandmother to each one of us. She handed the reins to Elmer, who had been first to reach the hitching post. Slipping off her horse she turned and asked with a mischievous twinkle in her eye, "Have you been good children?"

"Oh yes, yes," we shouted, crowding around her. One by one she gathered her parcels, finding something for each of us to carry. Like children following the Pied Piper, we trooped across the road and up the sidewalk to hotel porch, where we deposited her flowers, vegetables, and packages. Grandma walked slowly for she was very old, but she did not limp. When she was seated in her rocking chair, she reached for one of the bags and drew from it a huge round cookie with a big flat raisin pressed into the top. She repeated the gesture of drawing a cookie from her bag until we each had one. As she handed each child a cookie, she asked what we had been doing since her last visit. We reported whatever had been most exciting in the week past, and thanked her for our cookie. When the greetings were over we withdrew, leaving Grandma with her family.

When I first remember Grandma, she was already nearly ninety years of age. Though frail, she bore herself proudly. She spoke excellent English, having attended public school before coming to Fort Duchesne. My family knew her quite well. The Alfalfa Seed Experimental Farm was just across the river from her ranch, so my father had known her since the farm was established. Her daughters, Ethel and Mentora, were my mother's close friends. They lived at Fort Duchesne, and their children, Grandma's real grandchildren, were my classmates in the school at the Fort.

My earliest memory of Grandma was the day Aunt Phoebe took me, and her daughter, Gene, to visit Grandma's ranch. We walked on the trail which followed along the river for a mile or so. Crossing the highway, we turned into a tree-lined lane, which led to her small frame house. I was astonished to see growing 'round Grandma's door an exact replica of the rambling yellow rose I so admired on Aunt Phoebe's porch.

"Why, it's just like yours," I exclaimed, reaching out to touch a cluster of heavily scented yellow roses.

"Of course," Aunt Phoebe replied. "It was Grandma who gave me a cutting when we first came to live at Fort Duchesne."

Grandma waited in her doorway, holding the screen open for us. "Come in, I've been waiting for you and I've made some cold lemonade." She picked up a glass pitcher, and poured the lemonade into tall glasses. It was so welcome after our long walk. When we were seated she said, "I know you would like some of my chocolate cake." She lifted the cover from a glass plate, revealing a gorgeous cake covered with swirls of chocolate frosting. She cut generous pieces, putting them on china plates and handed one to each of us. Gene and I sat at the table eating our cake, while she and Aunt Phoebe settled in a pair of rocking chairs to visit.

Grandma's house was cool and spotlessly clean. The pine floor was scrubbed and shining. We were seated at a small table, covered with a white cloth and a centerpiece of fresh flowers. When we had finished our "tea," Grandma led us on a tour through her garden. There, we wandered among hollyhocks, asters, lilies, and daisies which were planted in rows like her vegetables. Growing along the border of the lane, were her famous roses, which Aunt Phoebe claimed were the most beautiful in the valley. Grandma Daniels had a reputation as a fine horticulturist. She won many prizes at the County Fair for her flowers. She was proud of her flowers, and shared them generously with Indians and Whites.

Everyone who knew Grandma was in awe of her, partly because she was so old, and partly because she was a living legend. I heard her story many times. Grandma was not born a Ute. She was born on the Navaho reservation, living near what was known as Lee's Ferry.

When Rose was about five years of age, she and her cousin were tending sheep in a box canyon on the Navaho reservation. It was near evening, and they were leading the sheep down the canyon toward home for the night. As they walked along, Rose said she heard a strange noise which she mistook for a flock of wild geese. Suddenly, they were surrounded by a group of men on horses. The girls began to run, but the warriors caught them and tied them to a tree, leaving them tied to the tree all night.

Next morning, that same band of White River Utes returned with many scalps hanging from their belts. They untied the girls, and took the girls away with them on their horses. Grandma Daniels never saw the Navaho reservation, nor any of her family again. Her captors took her to Colorado, where she lived as a slave with the White River Utes for two or three years. She tried to run away whenever she got the chance, but she was always recaptured and returned to the Ute camp.

Eventually, she was taken into the Uintah Basin, and sold to the Uintah Band of Utes. Chief Tabby took her into his household, where she lived for another two or three years, caring for his wife who was ill and disabled. When she died, Chief Tabby asked Rose whether she preferred to continue to live with the Indians, or go to live with the Whites. She said she preferred to go to the Whites, so she was taken to Fort Bridger, Wyoming. There, she was sold to Mr. Aaron Daniels, who was living at Fort Bridger with his wife and two daughters. Aaron Daniels was a member of the L.D.S. Church. His father had arrived in the Salt Lake Valley in 1847, with the first pioneers. Aaron and his first wife, Caroline, had been called to settle Utah Valley near where Provo was located. When gold was discovered in California, Aaron wanted to go to the gold fields, but Caroline did not want to leave the body of the Church. When she refused to go, Aaron married Harriett Nixon as his second wife, leaving Caroline and her children in Provo.

Aaron was a rancher, trapper, and prospector. He started up a ranch up the Uintah Mountains. Daniels Creek and Daniels Canyon are named for Aaron Daniels. He trapped in the canyon, and later found a gold mine. When he was told he had to give 10 percent of the gold to the L.D.S. Church as tithing he refused to do it, and apostatized from the church. He was working at Fort Bridger, as a scout and guide, when he acquired Rose to help his second wife, Harriett, and her two children.

Harriett accepted Rose into the family as a daughter and sister. After some time, they returned to Utah, living at Wanship for several years. Harriett left Aaron because of his heavy drinking. He went to live in Wyoming, and Rose was sent to Provo to live with Caroline.

Caroline was a cultured lady, who accepted Rose as her own. She taught her homemaking, cooking, cleaning, weaving, spinning, and sewing, all the skills necessary to make a comfortable pioneer home. Rose attended the Provo public schools with the rest of the Daniels children. After several years Caroline divorced Aaron, and in 1886 she married Abraham Owen Smoot. After the divorce, Rose was sent back to Aaron Daniels.

He took Rose with him to the Black Hills in South Dakota on a gold mining expedition. After a year they were driven from the area by the Sioux. They returned to the Tintic Mining District where Aaron worked as a miner, but moved from there to Ashley (now Vernal) in the Uintah Basin. When Rose was eighteen years old, she and Aaron were married at Blue Mountain, by Captain Pardon Dodds, acting Indian Agent. They made their home in Jensen, where their two sons, Hal Albert and Walter, were born.

The Uintah and Uncompahgre Reservations were consolidated at Fort Duchesne as the Uintah and Ouray Reservation. Congress passed an act in 1897, giving individual allotments of land to heads of Indian families. Captain Elisha W. Davis, Acting Agent at Fort Duchesne, helped Rose, who had been adopted by the Utes, apply for her portion. She was given one hundred and sixty acres on the Whiterocks Reservation, north of Fort Duchesne along the Uinta River.

Rose and Aaron cleared the land, and established a fine ranch where they grew a variety of fruits and vegetables. They raised chickens, horses, cows, pigs, and other animals. Two girls, Ethel and Mentora, were born to them making a family of four children. In 1896, eight years after they established the ranch, Aaron died. This left Rose to care for the children, and keep the ranch producing. He was buried on the ranch in a plot of ground east of the house and above the river.

Rose continued to live on the ranch. She set to work to make the land productive despite the blasting winds, grasshoppers and drought. She developed her own method of irrigating by lifting the water directly out of the river, and guiding it down the furrows of the garden. Year after year, she planted her vegetable garden, saving the best seeds in little jars. She experimented with many plants, trying many new varieties. She grew prizewinning vegetables and fruits on her farm. She successfully developed a lima bean that thrived in the short dry season of eastern Utah.

As the years went by, she cared for her home and children, making sure they had schooling until they all married and had children of their own. Rose lived alone in her little home, which was filled with articles of her own handwork, including the fine beadwork for which she was recognized. She took care of her horse, her four children, and her plants. She lived a long and busy life devoted to the care of others. She was the mother and grandmother of four children, twenty-five grandchildren, many great-grandchildren and all those children born to others that she cared for.

Rose died July 4, 1943. Funeral services were held in the LaPoint Ward Chapel of the Mormon Church, with Bishop George Hacking presiding. She was buried next to her husband in the family plot at the ranch. The inscription on her tombstone reads:

"Rose Daniels
1840-1943"

Everyone loved this small, brown Indian woman with the sparkling eyes known as "Grandma Daniels." She was a familiar sight on her old grey horse that plodded slowly, and made no sound in the soft sand of the Indian trail that wound along the river's edge shaded by the large willow and cottonwoods.

DINOSAUR BONES

Daddy at Dry Fork Canyon

In September, 1924, wagons carrying sixty thousand pounds of dinosaur bones passed through Roosevelt on the way to the University of Utah at Salt Lake City. They included bones of five complete specimens of dinosaurs which were to be assembled at the University, under the direction of Earl Douglass who had discovered them near Jensen, Utah, in 1909. My father had just begun teaching at the High School in Roosevelt, and had the opportunity to inspect the wagons. As an amateur geologist, he never forgot this experience, and never quit talking about it. As long as we lived in the Basin, the quarry in Jensen was his favorite place to take tourists, and in time that included me.

Douglass worked at the quarry for fifteen years after making his discovery. The site was declared a National Monument in 1915, but no permanent museum was established. However, the excavation of fossil bones continued. Though I was too young to remember that wagon train, dinosaur bones became an unforgettable part of my childhood.

"Dinosaur" means terrible lizard. Every time I walked to the post office at the Fort, I passed a dinosaur. Long before dinosaurs became part of children's culture, we played with a life-sized Allosaurus that was mounted on one end of a large storage building. It was a three dimensional model made of wood and canvas.

It was painted black with orange claws, and jagged white teeth. It protruded from the side of the building about sixteen inches, and was just wide enough so that we children could climb up onto it, and pretend the ferocious creature was alive. We held on to the jagged fins and rode off on our giant dragon to our imaginary adventures.

Broken pieces of fossilized bones lay scattered in the grass beneath the wood and canvas dragon. Half buried in the grass, they had probably been assembled as part of a U.B.I.C. exhibit at one time. For some reason they were never carried away, so we children invented a game to play with them. Like many of our games, it was a make-believe quest. We began our game sitting in a tight circle surrounding the pile of bones. Extending clenched fists, we counted out to determine who would be *It*. *It* had the privilege of choosing the site of our quest, and the magic weapon. Chanting this rhyme, we chose *It*:

> Dragon tail, dragon snout,
> Dragon wing, dragon spout.
> Who will drive that dragon out?
> One, two, three. Out goes he/she!

"You're *It* Leroy. You begin!"

"I'll catch that dragon 'n I'll kill him with my Magic Arrow!" He began by raising his pretend bow and sighting into the gooseberry bushes. "Must've been that dragon that killed John Pappas' sheep. I'm going to look down by the pump house." Leroy began, defining the rules and the scene for our game.

"Look at those huge tracks in the mud," I said, "they've only got three toes! It's a dinosaur! Look! The tracks lead up from the river."

"Yeah, it's headed for the hills," continued Bill, taking up the narrative. "I bet there's a cave up there. I'm not afraid to go after it. We've got the Magic Arrow. Who's coming with me?" And so on.

We took turns inventing the quest, until we cornered and vanquished our pretend dragon. Sometimes we sat in the circle, and pretended the whole game. More likely, we actually set off on one of those fantasy quests, dividing into teams of hunters and dragons. We set off across the fields to one of the nearby rock mesas which were pocked with caves, and well populated with lizards for our version of hide-and-seek.

Had we chosen the river bottom, we would have found trees left stranded on the sand bars. The tree skeletons became fortresses where we took refuge to defend ourselves while under siege. The rounded stones that littered the almost dry river bottom were natural cannon balls. We made catapults from willows growing along the river bank. Sometimes the trees became sailing ships for make-believe voyages to treasure islands. I don't believe rocket ships had been invented yet, or we'd have gone adventuring in them.

Dinosaurs came to inhabit the caves of the sandstone mesas where we played. They lurked in the shadows, and hid behind the red rocks. We believed that the small whiptail lizards that scurried over the rocks were enchanted, and that on dark and moonless nights they became full-sized dinosaurs again.

During the summer of 1934, my father's twin brother brought his family to visit us at Fort Duchesne. Uncle Carl, Aunt Oretta, and my cousins had never been in red rock canyons so we went to the Dinosaur Quarry. We drove by way of Randelett and Ouray so they could see the Green River Gorge. They were amazed by the water and wind sculptured landscape.

When we arrived at the quarry, which was located in the hills about five miles from the little village of Jensen, my father gathered us together in the shade for a lecture on geology. He pointed out the ledge above the bank of Green River where the huge skeletons were found. He explained how the mountains were formed, and how the valley was cut by the ancient river that deposited the dinosaurs in the mud so long ago. He led us along a rough shelf-like road cut into the mountainside, where weathered wooden ladders leaned against the ledge, and piles of shattered bones lay along the roadway. My father cautioned us not to step on them, as he led us along the road. We walked gingerly, avoiding the bones the same way we avoided stepping on graves in the cemetery. We were in fact walking in a graveyard. It was a graveyard for reptiles that had dominated the earth eighty million years ago.

The workmen let us examine the fossils, and we were quite properly amazed because some of them were huge. It was difficult for children to believe in the idea of extinction. It was easier to pretend invisibility, or changeableness, so we went on with our games. Pretending had been easy, but discovering reality was more difficult.

Fossil deposits were found in the Uinta Mountains by the first white explorers who visited them. In 1909, Earl C. Douglass of the Carnegie Museum, discovered a row of Brontosaur vertebrae in an exposed wall of sandstone below the mouth of Split Canyon, where the Green River cut through the eastern Uinta and Rocky Mountain masses. The south slope of Split Mountain is scarred by short deep canyons. Masses of grey shale are piled against the tilted layers of sandstone, known as the Morrison Foundation. These layers of hard sandstone and limestone resisted erosion by wind and water. Standing higher than the softer shales, which form the mass of the mountains, they were called hogbacks. The famous Dinosaur Ledge is one of the hogbacks that form a rim around Split Mountain.

Near the discovery site, Douglass built a five-room cabin. He lived there for fifteen years while he collected the fossil bones. He recruited men, horses, and equipment from nearby ranches to build a road leading to the discovery site. At the Dinosaur Ledge, Douglass made a cut more than a hundred feet long. At the base of the cut, he laid rails for small mine carts to haul away the debris of the quarry. Excavation continued during winter and summer. The work was done by hand with the help of local workers. The surface rock was shattered with dynamite. Then using hand drills, wedges, and crowbars, they removed large blocks of sandstone which encased the brittle fossil bones. They separated the fossils from the sandstone by hammer and chisel. They cut large blocks of bone-bearing material from the quarry. To prepare them for moving, they wrapped the blocks in strips of burlap dipped in flour paste. The casted bones were lowered by rope to a mule drawn skid and "snaked" them down the trail. The fossil bones were boxed in crates and hauled by freight wagons over sixty miles of rutted road to Dragon, Utah. There the cargo was loaded onto boxcars of the now abandoned Uintah Railway for transport to the Denver and Rio Grande line, and finally to the Carnegie Institute in Pittsburgh, Pennsylvania.

Douglass collected seven hundred thousand pounds of fossils, which included three hundred dinosaur specimens, two dozen of which were complete skeletons. Ten different species were represented. In nearly every museum of paleontology in the world where dinosaurs are displayed, there are bones of dinosaurs that were buried in Jurassic mud where Dinosaur National Monument now stands.

To protect the area for science, the quarry and surrounding land were declared a National Monument on October 4, 1915. Douglass worked at the quarry from 1909 to 1924. During the 1930's the monument served as a camp for transients. General development of the monument was carried on, financed by WPA funds, under the guidance of A.C. Boyle, resident geologist and custodian.

As long as we lived in the Basin, tours to the Dinosaur Quarry continued to be an exciting destination for tourists. But among my wintertime classmates, dinosaurs remained a subject to read about in encyclopedias. Dinosaurs were just another example of my imagination gone wild. Dinosaurs were resurrected after they were discovered by motion pictures and television for yet another generation to pretend about.

When I revisited Dinosaur National Monument, I saw nothing that resembled my childish image of dinosaurs. Remembered bones had diminished in size and quantity. The educational displays were interesting and informative, but devoid of romance. The quarry was covered with a modern building where we watched the workers through a glass window. The wild Green River which I had seen roaring through its deep gorge at Manila Pass had been tamed behind a nine-mile long Flaming Gorge Dam. Monstrous lizards no longer inhabited the rainbow hills. I preferred the old quarry from which I was permitted to select a small souvenir. It is a fragment of dinosaur vertebrae caught in a chunk of sandstone. I like to hold it on my palm like a talisman. It reminds me of our games, and the wonder of the child who walked among real dinosaur bones, colored stones, and quarry dust.

Leroy, ca. 1931

RUN SHEEP, RUNnn!

My children asked, "Where did you go, Mom?"
"Out."
"What did you do?"
"Ohh–nothin' much, we played games."
"Games?"
Probably the most exciting command I could think of at age ten was, "Run sheep, runnn!"

Games in the Alley

At Fort Duchesne, we had no television, no movies, no radio, no bicycle, and few toys, but we had space lots of space! Inside the Fort, the unpaved road swung in an arc around a large grass parade crisscrossed with walkways and shallow irrigation ditches. The houses faced the parade and towering over them a double row of cottonwood trees spread limbs to form a leafy arcade over the walks, the lawns and the road. Between each house a wide lawn extended between the buildings, and back to the alley. Some houses had shrubs planted around the large screen porches. Across the road was a large playground for children, tennis courts, and a baseball field for adults. All the buildings, lawns, and parade grounds were enclosed by a fence that marked the boundaries of the Fort. Only about a dozen children lived at the Fort, and when we played games children of all ages played.

The time for games was from after supper until curfew. After dark, the shadows cast by the trees and shrubs provided an infinite number of hiding places for hide-and-seek games. There was only one street light, and it served as our goal post. Moths and mosquitoes swarmed in a cloud around the one huge globe. Congregated in the lighted sand at its base were a hundred toads. From this center, joyous voices rang out nearly every night after supper to curfew, while our games spread over the wide lawns, the parade ground, and into the alley. The most exciting command was the ringing cry of "Run sheep, runnn!"

"Odds 'll be hiders, and Evens 'll be seekers," said Bob Litster, one of the older boys.

"One, two. One, two." We called, to choose sides.

Bob picked up a flat stick, spit on one side, and then tossed it into the air. "Wet or dry?" he said.

"Wet," shouted Bill.

"Dry," shouted Grant.

The stick spun up into the lamplight, then fell onto the sand.

"Dry!" Bob announced. "My team hides first. Now give me five minutes to hide my sheep. No one leaves the goal 'til I get back. Close your eyes 'n count to two hundred by fives. Come on sheep, follow me!" he said.

"Five, ten, fifteen, twenty ..." The Seekers leaned against the goal post, with eyes closed. Five sheep dropped into the shadows, and followed Bob into the alley behind Seeleys'. We huddled beside the woodshed while Bob gave us directions and signals.

"Here's your route. Go through Seeley's garden to the wood piles, then follow the fence, and cut through the alfalfa field behind Superintendent Tidwell's. Keep outside his yard! Stay in the irrigation ditch, and try to come into the goal from the trees by the tennis court. Remember, if you drop flat in the shadows and lie still, nobody can see you. Here are the signals: *Wolf* is danger, meaning lie low and hide; *Coyote* means move cautiously; *Red coyote* means move right; *Blue coyote* means move left. When I yell *Mountain Lion*, it means they're way off course. Keep moving, stay together, and don't run for the goal 'til I yell 'Run sheep, runnn!' Then run like hell!"

Bob left us and headed back to the goal. He drew a map in the sand with a stick, showing the spot he left his sheep. Bob followed the Seekers as they searched for his sheep, so he could call signals to guide us back to the goal without getting caught.

As soon as Bob left us, we ran toward the wood piles where cedar logs were stacked in rows like box cars. We slid into the shadows between two rows and crept toward the alfalfa field at the far side. The Seekers came into the alley.

"They went this way," said Grant. He crossed the alley, opened a gate, and led his team toward the wood piles out by the pump house.

"Wolf," Bob called. We dropped to our knees.

"They're not here," said Grant, "they must have gone up the alley." They searched the shadows by the woodshed, then the currant bushes on the lawn between Seeleys' and Naces' houses.

"Red coyote, red coyote," signaled Bob. We started to run. Halley tripped and squealed.

"They're in the field!" yelled Grant.

"Wolf! Wolf!" came the signal. We dropped flat in the field of alfalfa.

"Quit giggling." I jabbed Gene in the ribs.

"They went that way, up the alley," said Garth, and the Seekers started to run.

"Blue coyote," Bob called. We turned and crawled through the field on our bellies. We crossed the alley behind the other team and huddled in the slim shadows of Mrs. Tidwell's hollyhocks.

"Wolf, wolf, wolf," sang Bob softly. We tried not to breathe. Suddenly he yelled, "Red coyote!" We slithered into the long shadows of the tall trees, pressing flat into the damp grass. The Seekers beat the bushes around Burns' darkened house.

"Mountain Lion!" Bob yelled, "Mountain Lion!"

We scrambled to our feet, and raced across the road, dropping into the irrigation ditch just beyond the tennis courts. We lay there, panting.

"I heard 'em," said Leroy. "They're over by the tennis court!"

"Run sheep, runnn!" Bob commanded.

Panting and muddy, kids thundered toward the goal post, "We won, we won!" shouted the sheep as we fought to reach the goal before being tagged.

Next morning, Mr. Litster discovered the flattened path through the alfalfa field. It was a sober bunch of kids who listened to his sentence. He handed each of us a sickle, and sent us to harvest the damaged hay. If we were caught beyond the alley or fence, we were threatened with an eight o'clock curfew. Chastened by our public penance, we did our best to make amends, but for the rest of the summer our games were confined to the parade and the lawns. Even so, "Run Sheep, Runnn!" remained our favorite game.

Confined to the lawns between the houses, our games changed. *Pomp* became a favorite. Seeley's board sidewalk was used for one goal, and the next house down the line was the other goal. When playing tag, or hide and seek games, it is necessary that each player understands all the rules so there will be no cheating. Part of the game is making up the rules, such as: How do you tag? Where do you hide? What is meant by free? Defining the rules and giving handicaps to disadvantaged players, gives everybody a chance to play.

Choosing *It*, we counted out:

Onery, twoery, Dickory Dan
Washed his face in a frying pan
One, two, three. Out goes he/she!

Thus chosen, little Leroy stood at one goal, and the group at the other. "Pomp, pomp, pull away, run away, catch away!" he shouted.

Players made a dash for the opposite base. Pomp tried to catch the players. As soon as he tagged someone, they had to help him catch the others. The object was to be the last one caught, the first one caught became *It* for the next game. We played a variety of tag games that included *Kick the Can, No Bears Out Tonight,* and *Poison Tag.*

99

Boys and girls didn't always play together. Boys played marbles, which girls never did. Girls played jacks, and hopscotch which boys thought were sissy. Both played mumblety peg. Boys sometimes joined the girls at skipping rope. Often when boys turned the rope, they tried to trip the girls for a laugh. But the girls were much more skillful jumpers, and besides we knew dozens of jumping rhymes which were recited in a fixed order.

> Grace, Grace, dressed in lace
> Went upstairs to powder her face.
> How many boxes did she use?
(Count until a miss)
> Teddy Bear, Teddy Bear, turn around.
> Teddy Bear, Teddy Bear, touch the ground.
> Teddy Bear, Teddy Bear, button your shoe.
> Teddy Bear, Teddy Bear, Sit in your pew.
> Teddy Bear, Teddy Bear, climb the stairs.
> Teddy Bear, Teddy Bear, say your prayers.
> Teddy Bear, Teddy Bear, put out the light.
> Teddy Bear, Teddy Bear, say Good Night.
(Mime all the actions, then leave)

> Mable, Mable set the table.
> Don't forget the salt and PEPPER!
(Jump faster, and faster, until out)

A game we played often at the Fort, while we were waiting for it to get dark, was a game called STATUES. It was played on an open lawn. One player was chosen to be *It*, then all the other players huddled to decide what sort of action the statues would illustrate. For example, we might pretend to be building a house, or washing clothes on a scrubbing board, or chopping wood. *It* swung each player around by the hand saying:

> Statue, Statue take your form.
> Don't you move, 'til you are warm.
> Now freee—ze!
(and *It* let go)

The player staggered to a stop, assuming the position which mimed the predetermined action. The players remained "frozen" until all were positioned. Then *It* went around, and examined each statue trying to guess what action the statue illustrated. *It* could not touch the statue, but he could taunt the player and try to make him laugh, or "melt." *It* had a number of guesses, before moving on to other statues. As soon as a player melted, by moving, laughing, or falling down he moved to the sidelines where he joined the others, who had laughed. The sidelines jeered while *It* went on guessing the statues. The game was over as soon as all the statues had melted. Children like to be wild and unruly, even a bit crazy. The game Statues was fun to play because it provided a stage, and an occasion to be wild and out of control.

Another game with similar purpose was the game called Cheezit. It was a variation of hide-and-seek. Again, *It* was chosen by counting:

> One potato, two potatoes,
> Three potatoes, four,
> Five potatoes, six potatoes,
> Seven potatoes, more
> O,U,T, spells Out goes he/she.

It sat down on the front steps with ten fingers extended. Each player took hold of one of the fingers, and turned sideways facing the far end of the board walk. *It* started to count very fast, while the other players walked as fast as we could, "One, two, three, four, five, six, *cheezit!*" The players stopped instantly, "seven, eight, nine, ten *Apples.*" Most players kept walking. "Eleven, twelve *cheezit,*" someone was sure to keep walking, then he had to go back and start over. "Thirteen, fourteen little apples, fifteen, sixteen, *cheezit!* The player who got back to touch *It*'s finger could go hide. Gradually each player was hidden, then *It* had to go find the hidden players. While *It* was out seeking, the other players tried to return to the goal without being seen.

"I spy Leroy behind the lilac bush," *It* shouted, and they raced toward the goal. *It* got there first, "one, two, three for Leroy," *It* counted, touching the goal. Now out, Leroy joined the search.

101

Soon there were only a couple still hidden. *It* shouts, "ally, ally, OX in free!" All players raced to the goal. The last one to touch the goal was *It* for the next game. And so the games went on, and on.

"What did we do? Oh, nothing much, we played "Run Sheep, Runnn!"

Childhood is the time for games. We found our leaders, and followers, winners, losers and cheaters. There was no better way, not then, not ever!

Rainie

HAUNTED HOUSE

One of the houses at Fort Duchesne was haunted. It was locked up with the shades drawn. The government-issue furnishings were left undisturbed after Mrs. Nace died. Mr. Nace moved away and the apartment had not been reassigned. The children spread a rumor that it was haunted by the ghost of Mrs. Nace, who had been murdered. The rumor was embroidered into a fanciful tale that grew more gruesome with each telling. The buildings in the old army post were old and creaky, so it was that the children made up a reason to explain the vacancy. The tale contained all the elements of folklore, such as a lady in white who appeared suddenly, and without logical explanation. The ghost was real for the children. Stains on the old floor in the back room became blood stains, and ominous sounds and voices were heard from time to time.

Curiosity led the boys to investigate. They gained entry through a rear window, and we all sneaked in to look for ourselves. Inside, the shades were drawn so it was dark and spooky. Dust had collected on everything. In the kitchen, the water faucet dripped in the sink. The floor creaked. There were plenty of signs of mice, but no evidence of violence, and no blood stains. The cook-stove was cold and unfriendly. Dishes were still stacked in the pantry. A torn window shade flapped mournfully, and the door into the long dark hall sagged on a broken hinge. It was the kind of place that appealed to mischievous kids, so one of the intruders masterminded a practical joke.

"Hey," said Grant, "I've got a great idea."

"Yeah?" Halley challenged.

"Let's float a ghost down the front stairs."

"A ghost?" we chorused.

"Yeah. We c'n string a wire above the steps from the top of the stairs to the bottom," Grant explained. "We'll drape a sheet around a clothes hanger and slide it down the wire. It'll fly just like a real ghost!"

"What if we get caught?" Leroy asked.

"Ahh, no one will care," Grant said, brushing caution aside as he usually did. "Garth and Leroy c'n help me string the wire, Gene and Skinner c'n find a sheet and hanger."

The idea suddenly became a possibility. It even sounded like fun. We scattered to get the props, then returned to prepare the scene. Secretly, we completed the preparations. We even rehearsed it one afternoon. Our ghost billowed out and flew down the stairwell in a most convincing manner. What we lacked was a victim. The trouble was, that everyone knew about the ghost, except my baby sister, Lorraine, who was then about three years old. We knew we'd have to bribe her in order to persuade her to enter the dark and spooky house. So, we told her it was going to be a surprise party, and she was going to be part of the surprise.

After much persuasion we finally convinced her to cooperate. Gene and I dressed her in a clean dress and her Sunday shoes. We tied a new ribbon in her hair, and gave her a box wrapped like a birthday present to carry to the surprise party. We also had to keep Mama from being suspicious, so we told her we were rehearsing a play, which we were often doing since we made up most of our play activities anyway. I explained to Rainie what we were going to do while we walked up the row, past Seeley's, past a hedge of currants and raspberries to the haunted house. Only she didn't know about the house being haunted.

"Now there's nothing to be afraid of. We're gonna have a surprise party and you're gonna help make the surprise. You and I will stand between the front doors. When everything is ready, Leroy will whistle, then we'll open the doors and yell Surprise! That's all there is to it." I must have sounded very convincing, for she cooperated without much protest.

"But, why are we going to Nace's?" Rainie complained, "Nobody lives there."

"Because it's a very special surprise," I said. "Now just be quiet and I'll show you what to do." We approached the house, I took Rainie's hand and led her to the front porch. The boys had figured a way to open the front doors from inside, so we opened the outer pair of the double doors and Gene and I held Rainie in the small space between the inner and outer doors. Closing the outer door behind us, it was quite dark with the only light coming through the glass transom. Rainie began to whimper. "Shssh. . .," I said, putting my finger to my lips. "I can hear 'em. They've got the surprise all ready."

I knocked sharply on the inner door to let the conspirators know we were there. When Grant signaled, I was to throw open the doors, and he would send the ghost flying down the wire. About half a dozen kids were sequestered in the shadows to watch the fun. Gene and I waited in the dark, holding Rainie by the hand.

"Hsst!'" Grant's shrill whistle shattered the silence, and I threw open the doors. Light flooded the dimly lit hallway. A white ghost hovered on the top step of the stairs directly before us. Suddenly, it fluttered a bit, then flew straight toward us! No one screamed. There wasn't a sound. No one moved. Rainie simply fainted and fell in a lifeless heap at my feet. Then everyone began talking at once.

"What happened?"

"Is she breathing?"

"Is she dead?"

Lorraine lay motionless on the floor, with her eyes closed. I bent down to pick her up. She was very pale and limp as a rag. I became really frightened, for we couldn't rouse her. We thought we had scared her to death.

"We'd better take her outside," I said, pushing people away from her. My heart was pounding and my hands were shaking. "We'll have to tell Mama."

Leroy began to cry. I picked her up, carried her outside, and laid her on the grass behind the currant bushes. "What do we do now?" someone asked.

"I didn't mean to hurt her," Grant said, in a deflated voice.

"I'd better take her home to Mother," I said, repressing my tears. And with shaking hands, we wrapped her in the sheet that was used for the ghost.

"Here's my wagon," Garth said as he came running up the alley, pulling his little red wagon.

With heavy hearts, we lifted her into the little red wagon. We were a sorry bunch of kids as we trundled her along the bumpy sidewalk. Before we had gone more than a few feet, Lorraine began to cry. I burst into tears, too. The boys were scared stiff, but didn't dare run away. Mama met us half way. Seeing our remorse, she said nothing after we explained what we had done. Taking Rainie in her arms, she comforted her. "There, there," she said. "You're too little to play with the big children. They have more imagination than sense." She carried her into the house, and closed the door.

There were no more ghosts at Fort Duchesne for we had learned that "those who dance, must pay the piper."

SUMMER'S END: LOSS OF INNOCENCE

The Lab

Harvesting Alfalfa, Bob Hall at right

THE EXPERIMENT FARM

"Finish your breakfast while I do my chores," Daddy said. "I'll pick you up at the end of the alley." He picked up a pail, and went out toward the stables and garages to get his farm truck. Leroy and I needed no prompting. We were going to The Farm! The Uintah Basin Alfalfa Seed Experimental Farm was no ordinary farm. It was a laboratory. While Leroy struggled with his shoelaces, I ran to get my sun bonnet and the vegetable baskets. Mama stacked the dishes in the sink, and we trooped off to the cattle-guard at the end of the alley.

Daddy was waiting for us in the farm truck. One of the first models of pickup trucks, it was a Chevrolet with one seat, and an open wagon back. It had running boards, an adjustable wind shield, and no side windows. If it ever rained, there were leather flaps with isinglass windows to button in. The wheels had bright yellow wooden spokes and narrow tires. The truck belonged to the Experiment farm and was only used for farm business. Since we were going to the farm on business, we were permitted to ride in the truck.

"Let us ride in back, ple–ease?" Leroy and I begged together.

"Hang on!" Daddy said. He shifted gears and we were off.

I knelt down in back, hanging onto the spare tire which was attached to the side of the truck. Leroy knelt in the middle. Our heads barely reached above the top of the truck. Facing into the wind, I imagined myself to be a wild horse running over the prairie. Red sand spewed out from the singing tires, leaving a trail of pink dust storms as we galloped down the road.

The farm was located on US highway 40, about a mile north of Fort Duchesne and midway between Roosevelt and Vernal. Just beyond the metal bridge, which crossed the Uinta River, Daddy turned sharply to the left. Leaving the highway, he stopped at the farm gate. I jumped down to open it. Daddy drove through, and parked alongside a neat wooden building, called the "lab."

Compared to ordinary Basin farms, the Experiment Farm was very impressive. Its forty acres were completely fenced. A printed sign posted near the gate announced the farm's purpose and welcomed visitors. Inside the fence a road completely surrounded the farm. Grouped in the southwest corner, stood two round metal granaries and a low framed building, referred to as "the lab." Unlike other farm buildings in the Basin, the lab was finished with lapsiding, which was painted a cream color with white trim. It had glass windows which gleamed in the sunlight. The front door faced south, opening toward the highway. Two glass windows on either side of the door gave it the appearance of a very neat house, except that on the side of the low neat building were large double doors like a barn. They stood open, revealing farm machinery inside.

The farm fields were divided into plots about ten feet square. Narrow roadways and straight well-groomed irrigation ditches ran east and west, north and south, dividing the farm like a large checkerboard. Each plot was divided into rows planted with alfalfa and other crops. Garden vegetables grew scattered among the experimental plots of alfalfa.

Leroy and I often helped with weeding, and harvesting of garden produce. Sometimes we worked under Mama's supervision, for these plots were our family vegetable garden as well as part of the farm's experiments in testing new varieties of vegetables. Surplus produce was sold in bulk to local residents to help defray the cost of operating the farm.

The main purpose of the farm was to study the production of alfalfa seed, the most important crop in the valley. A variety of other crops were grown in order to determine what else could be grown commercially by the farmers in the Basin. These crops included melons, peas, beans and the first popcorn grown in Utah.

We followed Daddy into the building which served as warehouse, office, and laboratory. Inside, one entire wall was lined with shelves and bins for tools and supplies. Across the south end was the laboratory. Its wooden floor was raised one step above a larger area paved with gravel, where the farm machinery was stored during the winter. Beneath the windows was a work bench on which stood a microscope and a typewriter. Special cabinets held other instruments, and data books. There were several stools for the research assistants, who came from the college to work during the summer. The lab was kept very neat and clean. It was cool inside, and smelled of dry grass and gunny sacks. It felt like a very important place.

Mama selected a couple of hoes from the rack along the wall, and led us back outside. I took hold of one handle of a large wash-tub, and indicated to my little brother that he was to take the other side. We followed Mama to one of the plots.

"See those pig weeds," she said, pointing to weeds with red stems. "Now hoe them out carefully, so you don't cut the young shoots of corn. Work toward yourself, like this," she said, demonstrating for us.

I attacked the weeds with vigor, while she and Leroy went over to the pea patch with the tub. I felt very important working in the experimental garden, and tried to do the work without any mistakes. When we finished our assigned tasks, my brother and I would be free to play while waiting for our ride home.

Parked between the granary and lab were horse-drawn mowers, plows, and tillers, which we were allowed to explore. Leroy and I climbed onto the empty seats, and pretended to drive huge horses like those we saw in the horse-pulling contests during the U.B.I.C.. Bob Hall was a local farmer who worked at the farm, and supervised the crew of workmen. He laughed, and joked with us, while we mimicked his activities. We tried, without success, to shift the manual gears and brakes, and we shook the imaginary reins to get our horses to pull harder. Eventually, a gasoline-powered mechanical tractor and harvester replaced the horse-drawn equipment. First used and demonstrated at the farm, the new machines were objects of awe and admiration to all Basin farmers, who came to observe the work done at the farm.

Sometimes we were given special tasks to do. I especially liked being sent to fetch things from the granary, which stood next to the lab like a round metal tepee filled with sweet smelling seeds. Climbing into the bins, or scattering the seed was forbidden, but I could not resist sifting it through my fingers. Clean alfalfa seed is very beautiful. The seeds are like small hard grains of gold and like gold it glowed in the dim light. When disturbed slightly, the seed rolled down in sliding waves like fine dry sand.

Cutting Alfalfa

After I learned to read, I was given simple tasks in the laboratory. I cut tiny strips of paper to hold the stems of the alfalfa blossoms being prepared for the herbarium. Selected blossoms and stems were placed between layers of blotting paper, and strapped into a plant press to dry. The dried and flattened plants were mounted on stiff black paper, carefully labeled, and then taken to the herbarium at the college. I folded tiny paper boxes about an inch square, which were used in the greenhouse for planting individual seeds. I painted stenciled black letters and numbers on wooden labels, and paper bags. Though my tasks were simple, I learned to be accurate, patient and careful because I felt like I was doing important work.

The station entomologist, Mr. Charles Sorensen, kept his many trays of insects and butterflies in a special cabinet. One day when I was counting sacks, he stuck his head in the doorway, "Come outside Virginia, I have something I want you to help me with."

"What's that?" I asked as I walked out into the sunshine. Mr. Sorensen was holding something that looked like a fishing pole with a pillow case on one end.

"It's a butterfly net," he said. "Since you think so much of my specimens, I thought you might like to collect your own. I've fixed a cyanide bottle for you, and cleaned out a couple of old boxes. If you catch some nice specimens, and don't spoil their wings, I'll show you how to mount and label them. Let's go after that monarch," he said as he moved toward the field of flowering alfalfa.

"Oh, I'd love that," I said, my head filling with a vision of rows and rows of butterflies. During several summers, I collected butterflies, moths, and beetles. Mr. Sorensen gave me a big book with pages of colored pictures so I could identify them. I copied their names in tiny letters on the white paper that lined the wooden box. I stuck my dried butterflies on a pin, and placed them in the box. The neat rows of iridescent butterfly wings were like fragile jewels suspended in the paper-lined box. Priam's gold could not have been more pleasing to count, than were my rows of butterflies.

The work done at the farm was endlessly fascinating. Frequent visitors were enthusiastic about the work, too. Harvest, and threshing time, were the most exciting. Workers bustled about, while fantastic machines were made ready for public demonstrations. The big red threshing machine was run by pulleys and belts attached to a noisy gasoline engine. I never ceased being amazed that wheat loaded at one end blew straw and chaff out one chute, while seed poured into a sack attached to the other chute. The full sacks were sewn shut, and piled into a truck to be hauled to Roosevelt, where they would be cleaned and sold at Peppards Seed Company.

Harvesting lesser crops was rewarding, too. We helped fill large washtubs with green peas, bush beans, corn, beets, cucumbers, tomatoes, cantaloupes, and watermelons. These were distributed for sale from the farm warehouse, to Wong Sing's store, to farmers in the valley, and to families at Fort Duchesne. Much of the produce was preserved, and bottled in Mason jars by my mother for our family. They were stored in the back room, and transferred to Logan at the end of each season.

There was a weather station at the farm to record the temperature and humidity. It was read regularly each day, and the reading was recorded in a special book. Though this information was part of the experimental farm records, sometimes my brother and I were permitted to read the thermometer, hygrometer, and wind gauge so we could learn about the weather. Our readings were instructional only, the data we collected was kept in an orange school notebook. Data entered into the official record was read and recorded by the staff.

The Threshing Machine

In the summer of 1932, a variety of crops were planted to determine their commercial value for Basin farmers who had depended almost exclusively on alfalfa seed, and honey, as crops. Leroy and I were assigned a plot to grow flax seed. Daddy told us that if we were faithful to our task, we would be allowed to divide any profit from the seed between us. We had our hearts set on a new bicycle. As was Daddy's custom, we were expected to earn the first half, then he would match our contribution. This looked like a splendid opportunity, so we began the project with great enthusiasm.

I don't recall planting the seed, but when the flax began to grow, Leroy and I were charged with keeping it weed free. It was tedious work, for the flax seedlings were much smaller, and much less prolific than weeds. My grandfather had taught me how to tell the difference between weeds and seedlings when I helped him weed his garden in Logan. Confident that I knew how, I spent long hours sitting on a small, wooden stool, bending over the emerging flax and pricking out the small weeds. I was very proud as the flax began to grow. The plants were lacy and beautiful, and grew in straight rows. I waited anxiously for it to bloom. Buds appeared in clumps on the stems, and they began to swell, but still there was no color. An entry in my father's farm journal noted that the flax began to bloom on June 17th, which was Leroy's birthday. When the field came into full bloom, I was ecstatic. It was as if a patch of blue sky had fallen onto the field. Surely there would be bushels of seed. As the seed developed, and the flowers faded, we continued to pull weeds. Like the milkmaid in the fable, Leroy and I counted our golden reward before the harvest was realized.

As seed pods formed, the blue faded to the color of dry grass, and we prepared for our harvest. Daddy assembled the equipment needed to harvest, and collect the seed. It consisted of a wash tub, a scrubbing board, and scrubbers, which he had made by nailing pieces of rubber tire tread to blocks of wood. We used them to rub the seed out of its pods. First, we cut the tough stems with a sickle. Laying a small handful of flax on the board, I rubbed and scrubbed, until the seed and chaff began to collect in the bottom of the tub. There was much more chaff than seed, and we had to pick this off, or blow it away from the seeds. Leroy was extremely allergic to the dust and pollen, so much of the harvest depended on my efforts alone. I lost much of our valuable seed on the ground, while I was cutting the flax. And I lost even more of it when we emptied the tub onto a screen resting on a pair of saw horses over another tub from which we dipped the seed into muslin bags. The harvest was slow and tedious, as well as dusty and dirty. As we collected seed, we piled the stocks for straw. The tops of the bags were sewed closed and numbered tags attached. Daddy was proud of our success and pleased that we had finished our task. He sent the seed to the Peppards Seed Company for it final cleaning and sale.

I do not remember how many pounds of seed were sown or harvested. But when our check arrived the following spring, we had the forty dollars necessary to buy the big blue balloon-tired bicycle that Leroy and I had longed for. The flax harvest ended our experiments at seed growing. I had learned from this experience how difficult it was to see a project to its end, and how important it was to use care if the product were to retain value for others.

The investigations at the Uintah Basin farm never solved the problems of growing alfalfa seed for the local farmers. In 1935, the farm was reluctantly abandoned, because no satisfactory solution to the problems of seed production had been found. The lease on the farm had expired, and the search for a solution would continue in the various schools of agriculture under the direction of the United States Department of Agriculture. It would take another forty years of patient research, breeding new strains of alfalfa, the development of adequate insecticides, and the development of proper cultural practices, before success could be claimed.

From my father's work at the Uintah Basin Alfalfa Seed Experimental Farm, I learned the value of dedication to an idea which he believed to be true. I learned the value of patience, of results, of careful observation, of delayed judgment, and most important, of the need for integrity in one's labor. I learned that discovery is never the result of one man's work. Rather, it is shared labor, and shared knowledge. I also learned that work undertaken with a purpose is a pleasure, and often its own reward. With the passage of time, respect and honors came to my father, but in his daily work he found his own joy, pride, and satisfaction. In the last year of his working life, he witnessed a totally successful harvest resulting from the application of his theories for successful production of alfalfa seed in his own field.

The New Tractor

*A slightly different version of this story "Growing Up on an Experimental Farm," was published by the Utah State Historical Society in *Beehive History, 9, c1983.*

THE U.B.I.C.*

Boom! Boom! Rat-a-tat tat! The snare drums struck a marching rhythm. The color guard led the Grand Parade with the Stars and Stripes, followed by the 38th Infantry Band from Fort Douglas, in Salt Lake City. The Band struck up a lively Sousa march for the occasion. Next came the officials, and visiting dignitaries in shiny open touring cars. Riding close behind rode mounted Chiefs of the Uintah, White River and Uncompahgre bands of the Ute tribes dressed majestically in full regalia. They carried ceremonial spears, and their horses were caparisoned in beaded saddle-blankets, and silver-trimmed harness. The Uintah and Duchesne High School bands, the 4-H Clubs, and all the Boy Scouts in the valley marched in uniform. The famous "Six Horse Hitch" from the Ogden Union Stockyards brought up the rear. The parade, scheduled for 10 o'clock each morning, assembled on the ball park, and marched entirely around the Fort, while waving spectators cheered from the sidelines. It was a spectacle like no other.

Of all the events of summer, none took precedence over the Uintah Basin Industrial Convention. To label it the Basin's greatest institution was hardly an exaggeration. Conceived as a self-help solution to failing crops, and the problems of establishing a thriving local economy, it succeeded beyond belief. In August, much of the Basin's population of twenty thousand people, gathered at Fort Duchesne for three days of educational recreation. The convention was a combined school and festival, where white settlers and Native Americans came together to learn the latest developments in scientific farming, and home economics. Combining learning with entertainment, the people in the Basin were joined in this big family gathering by professionals from Utah's universities, various government agencies, and private businessmen, who eagerly shared in the development of Utah's great "Inland Empire."

The U.B.I.C., as it was affectionately called, lasted three days and nights. But for the residents of Fort Duchesne, the excite-

117

The 38th Infantry Band from Salt Lake City

ment lasted much longer. Planning for the event went on all year. Volunteers spent weeks in preparation. The festivities utilized every inch of the former military post. By July, the exhibit halls were opened and cleaned, and folding tables and chairs were set up for classes. Half the parade ground was converted to a large campground. Campsites were provided with stacks of cedar firewood, and huge wooden boxes for trash. River stones were arranged for fire pits. Workers brought a small forest of logs from the mountains, to construct a stage and benches for the outdoor theater. They built a dance floor and strung it with electric lights. The old bandstand was draped in red, white, and blue bunting.

Children's Playground, U.B.I.C.

The bandstand served as the convention center. They fenced the playground for small children. Other areas were prepared for games and athletic events of all kinds. The ball park, bleachers, and horseshoe pits were readied for games and contests. Booths, to sell foods of all kinds, were built in a row along the lower side of the parade. In the corner next to the tennis courts, a large tent was transformed into a soda fountain. It was complete with little round tables and wire chairs. Ice cream sodas, root beer floats, banana splits, orange crushes, and lime rickeys were dispensed for a nickel. Ice cream sundaes cost a dime. The firehouse doors were thrown open and the nickel-plated pumper was polished. The hoses had been tested, and the marvelous machine visible only on this occasion stood at the ready.

The carnival excitement climaxed with the arrival of Native

Americans, who came to make their camp in the river bottom, where they pitched tents, and built temporary corrals. The military band from Fort Douglas, was bivouacked in one of the old barracks. Families came from all over the valley. Some pitched tents in the campground, while others occupied spare beds, and improvised space in the apartments of the permanent residents. Every available bed and sleeping porch was utilized by friends, families, and visiting dignitaries.

The Bandstand, U.B.I.C.

The events listed in the program for 1932, were typical. Festivities began at sunrise with a bugle call. The flag was raised at seven o'clock. The smell of frying bacon rose in a cloud over the breakfast fires, as the celebrants prepared for a busy day. At our house, children were spread out on the floor of the sleeping porch. Breakfast was served at a makeshift table set up on saw horses in the back room.

Children saved their pennies for weeks. Many pennies had been earned running errands during the weeks of preparation. They were spent during the festival on games of chance, for ice cream cones, licorice whips and other treats that were unavailable at other times.

Each day, following the parade, activities continued at a heady pace. Simultaneous events included a horseshoe pitching contest and a horse weight-pulling contest where farmers compared their teams. Baseball games were serious contests, for the Utes had a champion team. Field events, oratory, and community singing filled any gaps in activities.

Throughout each day, a full schedule of classes was offered in such subjects as Forest, Range, and Livestock Management, Farm Mechanics, Feed and Food Crops Production and Clothing and Food Preparation. A Health Clinic, and a Better Babies Contest were held for both White and Native American mothers. Tours of the Alfalfa Seed Experimental Farm were featured. In the Children's Playground, recreation specialists from the universities supervised games, and contests for young children. Home Reading, Storytelling, Handicrafts, Folk Dancing, and Youth Leadership activities occupied the older children. Daytime assemblies, and evening programs, featured guest speakers from the universities in Utah, and various government agencies. The Governor, and the Commissioner of Indian Affairs gave speeches. Awards and prizes were presented at each evening program. There were medals, ribbons and trophies for nearly everyone. Late evening entertainment provided a choice of an outdoor picture show, or dancing to the music of a local dance band. The U.B.I.C. was universally enjoyed. All who came shared the determination to improve their opportunities, and to have fun doing it. No one went home uninformed. No other event evoked a greater sense of kinship, and hope.

My brother, Leroy, and I, looked forward with great anticipation to our young house guests. Included were the children of Erastus Peterson, Uintah County Agent, and the children of the Edwards, Dillman, and Orser families from Roosevelt. The boys went off to games of skill and woodcraft and the girls to various homemaking events, while the little ones were entertained in the playground.

I remember best one event that held the greatest enchantment for me. Like a veritable royal feast, Lottie K. Esplin spread her story books across a magic circle of green felt which she called her "book table." The children, seated round her table, had never seen such fare. In the frontier towns of the Uintah Basin, there were no libraries and no bookstores. There were only two movie theaters, and even a radio was rare. On her book table, Mrs. Esplin, Home Reading Specialist for the Utah State Agricultural College

Extension Service, displayed a collection of choice books which she shared through reading and storytelling with the children attending the U.B.I.C.. They included selections from the most recent books published for children. There were stories of adventure, make-believe, biography and far away places. At week's end, the books were offered for sale. That book ladened circle of felt was the beginning of the fine bookstore Mrs. Esplin later established in Logan. She called it The Book Table. I still have books my mother bought for me from that felt table. They include the D'Aulaire's *Miki*, Carol Ryrie Brink's *Caddie Woodlawn*, Rachel Field's *Taxis and Toadstools* and *Little Faces From Far Places.*

The horse-pulling contest was a popular event for both farmers and spectators. The "Six Horse Hitch" team from Ogden was pitted against locally bred teams. The horses' manes and tails were braided with red, white and blue ribbons for the occasion. The powerful teams were hitched to a triangular sled which had a huge stone weight suspended a few inches above the ground. With muscles straining, the horses struggled against the dead weight, bracing their huge feet and blowing through their massive nostrils. As the sled began to move, the weight dropped with a grinding thud while the horses dragged the sled along the runway. The teams were judged for form, weight, and the distance the dragged the weighted sled. A new harness, cash prize, and trophy were awarded to the best team. At that time, farming depended on horse power, so farmers displayed their trophies with great pride.

I saw my first moving picture show during the U.B.I.C. Several bed sheets were sewn together to make a screen, which was stretched between two large trees growing next to the tennis courts. Folding chairs were set up for the audience. We children sat on the ground in front of the chairs. The little children were in front, and the taller ones were behind. Spectators gathered long before sundown waiting for it to get dark, so the show could begin. The air reeked with the smell of citronella, which we rubbed on our bare arms and legs, hoping to discourage the mosquitoes. Finally, it grew dark enough, and the projector began to roll. There come to life on that makeshift screen, was the saga I had heard about since infancy. Pioneers rolled across the screen in creaking ox-drawn covered wagons. There, were the women in sunbonnets and the men in buckskins, trekking over the prairie in a cloud of dust, while heroic Jim Bridger led the way. *The Covered Wagon* was a monumental film. Made in 1923, it portrayed all the amazing adventures and hardships of the pioneer men and women who opened up the western wilderness to White settlement. It was also a significant movie, because every bit of it was filmed out-of-doors. It portrayed a fight with Native Americans, a nine-mile prairie fire, the fording of a river, and a genuine buffalo stampede. Since this first western epic had been filmed on the wide-open prairie, it was appropriate to view it under the open sky.

The "Moving Picture Show"

This great adventure, directed by James Cruze, was filmed on the western Nevada desert ninety miles from a railroad. Five thousand actors, including two thousand full-blooded Native Americans, worked four months to film this cinematic masterpiece. Much of it was filmed in Snake Valley, Nevada, but the buffalo stampede was filmed on Antelope Island in the Great Salt Lake. *The Covered Wagon* ran for two years on Broadway, thirty-four weeks in Los Angeles, twenty-three weeks in Chicago and for three starry nights at Fort Duchesne, to what I am sure was its most appreciative audience.

The first U.B.I.C. grew out of necessity. In 1923, many of the Basin homesteads were on the verge of failure. Production of alfalfa seed and honey had declined. Transportation of alfalfa hay was too expensive for Basin farmers to compete in the market-place. They needed new crops, and a solution to alfalfa seed failure. The Uintah Basin Industrial Convention came into existence as a cooperative effort of self-help, and reeducation. It was a grassroots effort to maximize the resources of the valley.

The first Committee included Fred A. Gross, Superintendent of the Uintah and Ouray Agency, Mary Orser, and Ray Dillman of Roosevelt, Erastus Peterson of Vernal, Phoebe C. Litster, and Johnny Victor of Fort Duchesne. They planned the convention to renew morale of the farmers, to pool resources, and for the farmers to rededicate themselves to success.

The second U.B.I.C., in 1924, was promoted statewide by the publication of a booklet entitled, *The Happy Homeland.* Each community produced a section which described the Inland Empire in glowing terms. It expressed the faith, hope and aspirations of twenty thousand people, who had settled in the valley of twenty-five thousand square miles. The pride of the people rings out in the glowing prose used to describe their valley:

". . . These pages tell the story of the great Uintah Basin Industrial Convention, with its annual conclaves of brains, scientific research and demonstrated facts. . . . Stories coming from behind mountain barriers a hundred miles from railroads, markets and competitive enterprises, read like fairy tales. . . . Here the mighty mountain torrents are transformed into silvery streams . . . changing deserts into rose gardens, sage brush flats into alfalfa fields, and sand dunes into orchards."

Ten years later, when the U.B.I.C. of 1932, came to an end, the Committee decided to discontinue the event. At their final meeting, a mass of Basin citizens turned out to protest. A new administration at the Agency was persuaded to let the popular festival continue, and a date was set for the following year.

Participation of the Native Americans in the U.B.I.C. changed as Native American policy changed. In the beginning, Ute culture was authentically represented. Gradually, the dances and pageant became glamorized for the white tourist audience. In 1933, the Indian part of the program was a dramatic presentation of Longfellow's poem *Hiawatha* featuring Uintah and Ouray Utes. The Native Americans were not satisfied.

For the U.B.I.C. 1934, Mildred Dillman of Roosevelt, who was a recognized scholar of Ute culture, wrote a pageant which portrayed Ute history and culture. This pageant was directed by Lester Chapoose of Whiterocks. It featured Native Americans in native costumes. Interpreters translated the Ute dialects which were spoken by members of the different bands who performed in the pageant. Between scenes, authentic ceremonial dances were performed, to the accompaniment of Native American musicians.

In spite of the effort to present authentic Ute culture, the U.B.I.C. of 1934 was marred by tragedy. Three people were shot, bringing the celebration to an untimely end. In September of the same year, the first "Indian Fair" was held. The U.B.I.C. was to be discontinued because the new administration saw it as competitive and divisive. Given the economics of the Depression and the politics of the New Deal, the U.B.I.C. seemed an unnecessary extravagance because it required so much time and energy of Agency personnel. Conflict between Native Americans who held to the old ways, and those who followed the White man's law was growing, creating problems for the Administration.

Aunt Phoebe, who had served on every U.B.I.C. committee since 1923, said, "I believe it was the best thing ever done for the Indians, because it did not set them apart from other citizens of the Basin community. The U.B.I.C. was an institution that died of its own success."

No one who participated in a U.B.I.C. during those years would dispute Aunt Phoebe's conclusion. The gathering had provided entertainment for whole families together, while it brought hope and good cheer during very difficult times. It had also provided an opportunity for real education in a very isolated region. It seems doubtful that any child who attended that wonderful celebration has ever had a better time anywhere. None of the children forgot the sights the sounds the smells the festival celebration!

*Uintah Basin Industrial Convention began in 1923.

Indian Dancer

After the Parade
Courtesy of L. C. Thorne Collection

Ute Chiefs and Dancers

Chief John Duncan
Courtesy of L. C. Thorne Collection

John Victor, 1934

MY JOHNNY

Soon after I started school, Johnny and Marie moved to the cottage next to the entrance gate. The cottage was closer to the administration building where Johnny worked. There he had a fenced yard with a turnstile gate, and a big screened porch. I continued to visit him frequently on my way to the Post Office to get the mail from our box.

One day I stopped at Johnny's, and found his porch filled with tables piled with feathers and beads, drums, and Native American artifacts. Johnny told me that he was going to be one of the dancers in the Indian Pageant that Aunt Bill [Mildred Dillman] had written. He and Marie were making costumes for the dancers. As I watched him adding beads and feathers to his costume, I became quite excited. He said I must wait until the performance to see his costume, because there would be special music and dancers, also.

Preparations for the U.B.I.C. required every worker at Fort Duchesne. In the center of the old parade grounds, workmen constructed a stage. Pine logs were brought from the mountains, and piled criss-cross to raise a platform over which the dance floor was laid. Willow and aspen boughs formed the background of the stage. Colored electric lights were hung between the trees and along the front stage for footlights. Rows of logs provided seats for a large audience. As preparations stretched over several weeks, anticipation grew. Finally, everything was ready.

On the first night of the Pageant, the assembled audience seated on the log benches waited expectantly. The program began with a band concert. The band played until it was quite dark, then the stage was cleared to make ready for the Pageant. The tall trees growing on either side of the stage extended it into the darkness so that the stage appeared to be much larger than it really was. In the eastern sky, a silver moon reinforced the make-believe world. The footlights were turned on. Native American drummers sat around a large drum located to one side of the stage. Behind the drum, the singers and flute players sat cross-legged before the forest background. A Native American woman, who was to be the reader for the pageant stood before a microphone.

The drums sounded the ancient rhythm, beginning softly as the reader began to speak. Then the rhythm of the drums changed, building to an exciting crescendo. The singers began to chant, and suddenly the figure of a man appeared in the spotlight. His arms were held high and his legs were spread wide; he looked like a giant bird. Beaded leggings covered his legs above ornate moccasins, and a quill breast plate gleamed on his bare chest. An eagle bonnet spread out from his painted face, the white feathers sweeping down his back to touch the very ground. A single gasp silenced the crowd.

The music changed rhythm, and the figure moved slowly forward, followed by a line of dancers. As the dancers moved closer, my heart leaped to my throat. I could not believe what I saw. Transformed into this magnificent creature was my Johnny*!*

The dancers spread across the stage, while the quavering voices of the singers chanted in rhythm with the throbbing drum. The feathers of the great eagle bonnet spread like wings, soaring with the music. I could hardly breathe. Never had I imagined such sounds! Never had I seen such splendor!

I shall never forget that electrifying moment when I recognized My Johnny. Dancing before me was a magnificent and magic figure. He was glorious, exalted, and powerful! My own heartbeat adjusted to Johnny's lifting and falling feet. As I watched, I felt the pride with which he bore the majestic eagle bonnet. I watched his face, and sensed his rapture. I watched the heroic dance, and I knew what it meant to be *Indian.*

"Oh Johnny, My Johnny! What have they done to you? Why did you trade your buckskins and eagle bonnet for blue jeans and a working shirt?" I cried to myself. I would never be able to look at Johnny with clear-eyed innocence again. Though I watched Johnny dancing on a stage, and not in the ceremonial circle, I understood what it meant for a Native American to dance. For him, his dance was the supreme expression of his belief and desire. Only then, was the Native American whole and beautiful. It is no wonder the borrowed clothes of the white man seemed awkward. They were a sham, and a betrayal. They diminished the Indian and made him invisible to white men. That knowledge made me ashamed of my own tribe. Shame became guilt.

The Pageant continued. The drama depicted the history of the Utes, and the settlement of the valley. The Native Americans spoke in their various dialects, and their parts were translated for the White audience.

Mrs. Dillman reminded me of the Pageant, but I remembered nothing of the rest of the program. Since that night, I have carried in my heart the image of Johnny dancing. It pains me that there is another image, also. I never told him how I felt. How could I? When I tried to explain to my family how I felt, I was reproached for loving him. I was told that I was just being a childish romantic, and that my feelings were unsuitable. When we left Fort Duchesne, Johnny and I parted as friends, but we remained sojourners of alien worlds. He was a man, who happened to be a Native American, and I was a child with white hair, fair skin, and blue eyes who came to live next door.

After we moved away from Fort Duchesne, I did not return until the summer of 1944. I had not kept my promise to come for the Bear Dance in the spring. My father had business in Roosevelt, and he drove us to see the Fort once more before my brother went into the Navy. He drove quickly around the circle of the Fort. It was greatly changed. Paint peeled from the old buildings. Rusted screens sagged. Windows were broken. We looked away as we passed the building that had been home. Our friends were gone. I never saw Johnny again.

Aunt Bill knew Johnny. She had written the *Indian Pageant* in which he danced. When I went to see her in 1977, she reminded me of that, and she showed me colored slides. They were pictures of him on his horse. He was wearing his regalia, and carrying a shield and spear. In another picture, he stood by a log in a grove of aspen trees tall and massive like a bear in beaded leggings.

Aunt Phoebe told me that he lived to be an old man. He never had children of his own, but he raised his brother's sons. He was honored in his tribe as a dancer, and Chief Singer for the Ute's traditional Bear Dance. I too, honored Johnny, but I had not told him so.

Belatedly, I confess my love for John Victor, and his gentle Marie. I regret my silence, for I have at last come to understand. It was Johnny and Marie who taught me that the color of eyes and skin are accidents of birth, of heritage, and of geography. From them, I learned that in the life of the spirit, and in the experience of the heart, all men are the same. We are indeed brothers. I hope that "My Johnny" knew he was my elder brother. I shall remember him dancing, in an eagle bonnet and feathers. They suited him well.

BLACK EYES AND BLUE EYES MEET

On the last evening of the U.B.I.C. in 1934, I sat with friends waiting for the pageant to begin. Darkness gathered slowly. Stage lights flickered from the brass instruments as the conductor raised, and then lowered his baton. The mellow music of the brass choir dissipated the day's energy and excitement into the fading twilight. The audience sat on log bleachers, facing the stage. Chatter stopped, and the restless audience grew quiet while the band played. Suddenly a voice over the loudspeaker demanded that the doctor and Superintendent Page go to the Camp behind the hospital. The band music resumed, but the mood was gone. Restless curiosity spread through the crowd, and the band changed to a livelier tune, then stopped altogether. The presentation of awards began.

There were awards and trophies for the horseshoe pitching contest, the singles tennis, archery champions, the better babies and Boy Scout merit badges. The loudspeaker interrupted, announcing that the rest of the performance would be canceled. News of gunfire in the Native American Camp spread through the assembled audience like wild fire. Someone had shot three people, then escaped! Horror gripped the audience which broke up in confusion and dismay. Spectators were instructed to return to their campsites and homes. Further instructions would be issued as soon as possible. Whites hurried toward their buildings. Native Americans scurried toward their campgrounds behind the hospital. The flaring lights of lanterns sent flashes of fear in all directions.

Leroy and I were sent upstairs to bed, but we did not sleep. We plastered our noses against the window screen of Daddy's office, and watched the activity in the field that separated the row of houses from the hospital. The window overlooked the hospital grounds, where confusion reigned. A light went on in the canvas wailing tent, casting weird shadows as figures moved inside. Muffled shouts were mixed with night sounds as we watched the frenetic activity. Eventually, Mama came to pull the shade and close the window, sending us to bed.

Next morning a notice was issued, explaining that a Native American, called Mountain Lion, had entered the tent of a family who had come to the U.B.I.C. There was a fight. Two Indians had been shot dead, and a third was wounded. Mountain Lion had escaped, and the sheriff's posse had gone to look for him.

Daddy said that what had happened was none of our business, and we were warned to stay away from the hospital, until the matter was settled. Rumors spread and fear took over. Panic brought the U.B.I.C. to an untimely end. Families packed up and fled from the Fort.

Mama was adamant that we remain confined to the house and yard. Leroy and I posted ourselves in the office window, where we had a front row seat to observe the events unfold. From our window we watched as people dismantled their tents, packed up and left the U.B.I.C. campgrounds. Everything was a shambles, as people hurried to get away.

Eventually, the facts became known and were published in the newspapers. Mountain Lion, a fifty-seven-year-old Indian, had entered the tent of the mother of his former wife, where she and his two year old son were staying. The young Native American woman, named Stella Yump, had been given to Mountain Lion for a bride by her father. She had left him several weeks before for a younger man named Henry Johnson. Stella and Henry ran away and were married under the white man's law. They had come to the U.B.I.C. and were all staying in the same tent. Believing Stella still belonged to him, Mountain Lion entered the tent wielding a club with which he threatened to kill Henry. A struggle ensued. The club was wrested from him. Mountain Lion then drew a revolver, and began shooting. He shot Henry through the heart, and wounded Stella's mother. Stella ran from the tent and Mountain Lion followed her. About fifty yards from the tent, he fired a shot which killed her. Mountain Lion fled into the darkness of the river bottom. Henry and Stella were declared dead and their bodies were taken to the death tent next to the hospital, where arrangements were made for their burial. The wounded woman was admitted to the hospital. At daylight, a posse set out to track Mountain Lion.

Families who had come to the U.B.I.C. left the Fort. Everyone who lived at the Fort was preoccupied with this horrible happening. From the vantage point of our upstairs window, my brother and I watched the events being played out on the field below us. We watched the Native American women who came to grieve. They knelt beside the wailing tent, their hair was shorn, and they rubbed themselves with ashes. Kneeling beside the tent, and rocking back and forth to the rhythm of their mournful song, they wailed loudly in the anguish of their grief. This continued throughout the day, as tribal and agency officials came and went from the hospital grounds. Gradually the mourners withdrew.

Shortly before sundown, a farmer living about five miles from the agency, reported that he had seen a body hanging from a tree. News spread quickly. Everyone assumed that it was Mountain Lion's body, and there was a sigh of relief that there was no mad man out there gunning for us.

Rumor was rampant among the Fort's residents. We children were simultaneously repelled, and drawn by curiosity. We watched the sheriff's truck leave the Fort, and we assumed they had gone to retrieve Mountain Lion's body. From the vantage point of the upstairs window we watched for its return. Sometime later, the truck drove up the back alley and parked behind the hospital. Sheriff Seeley went into the hospital, leaving the truck unattended.

Leroy and I sneaked down the stairs, and made our way to the irrigation ditch in the field beside the hospital. There we found the Seeley boys who had the same idea. Together we crouched in the ditch and waited to see if anyone had noticed us. Compelled by curiosity, we crept along the ditch toward the truck, crawling through the tall grass and fearfully moving closer to the truck. We snaked under the barbed wire fence, and entered the forbidden hospital grounds. As we approached the parked truck, we became aware of another group of intruders. Our Native American playmates had slipped through the bushes on the other side of the field, and were creeping toward the truck also.

I can still see the two rows of heads lined up on either side of the truck. On one side a row of blue eyes peered over the bed of the truck, and on the other side, a row of black eyes peered back. For a brief moment our eyes met, then we averted our gaze, and glanced uneasily into the truck bed. Lying on a bed of sacks was a body wrapped in a canvas shroud. Beside it lay a noose of barbed wire wound with a red silk neckerchief.

Too shaken to run, I stood paralyzed, stricken with sudden knowledge. Stung by the recent memory of Johnny dancing, and the horror of Mountain Lion's revenge, I realized how great was the gulf that separated the White and Native American children who stared at each other over that awful cargo. No longer innocent children who played together and went to school together, we had become aliens with differing cultures. We were products of our heritage.

"What's going on here?" demanded John Victor, who had discovered us peering into the truck. My heart sank, and I stared at Johnny's feet, ashamed at being discovered.

"Nothing," we chorused, terrified at having been caught. Nothing? How did we know what to think, or what was going on? We had suffered shock. We were afraid, and no one had explained anything to us. We were staring at a corpse that by white man's law and custom was the shrouded body of a murderer! Yet instinct told us that was not the whole truth.

John Victor was an Uncompahgre Ute. He served as the Native American policeman for the Agency. He was also the official interpreter between the Indians, who spoke different dialects, and the White officials who had authority over all the Native Americans, yet spoke only English. Because of this, Johnny knew better than anyone about the failure of language, and the clash of cultures. Besides, Johnny was a special friend to all of us and none of us feared him. There was no anger in his voice when he sent us away. He spoke with tight-lipped resignation as he said, "It's time for you to go now. We'll take care of this."

The knowledge that Mountain Lion's body had been brought back to the Agency resulted in further excitement in the community. However, in due time, the body was prepared for burial. Mourning at the death tent resumed.

A day or two later, Henry Johnson's father appeared and an

inquest was held at the Agency. We learned that under Native American custom, he had the right to determine the manner of Mountain Lion's punishment. Speaking to the mourners, Henry's father said that by taking his own life, he believed that Mountain Lion had paid for the life of his son, Henry. He was satisfied. The matter was finished. Things should go on as before.

Whites viewed Mountain Lion's death as a suicide, but the Native Americans believed differently. They knew that Mountain Lion had behaved according to traditional belief, and acted according to the primitive custom of his ancestors. Stella had been given to him by her father. Stella and Henry had violated a tribal custom, so the betrayed husband sought the revenge that was his right by custom. In order to expiate the shame brought to his family, Mountain Lion sacrificed his own life.

After a few weeks the event was forgotten. For me, however, things did not go on as before. My perception had been altered by these events. I became painfully aware of the differences between Native Americans and Whites. We children had been terrified by this murder in our own neighborhood. A shroud of silence was wrapped around the whole affair, so that none of us could ask questions, or discover any means of understanding the event. My relationship with Johnny was changed, and I became aware of taboos in my own Mormon family. I was troubled, but because my father did not want to intrude into what he believed was the Agency's business, I was forbidden to ask questions that would have helped me understand. I had witnessed the power of passion. I wanted more than anything to understand, but I was hushed into silence. I was told that the events were none of my business. But that did not explain the events. By imposing silence upon me, my elders made me conscious of color, of race, of class, and of prejudice. I took upon myself guilt for the ignorance and prejudice exhibited in my own family. The memory of this experience remained, and I did not discover a satisfactory explanation until I encountered a Native American scholar who explained it to me many years afterward.

The Ute symbol of death is a spread eagle with a red triangle against the black body. The wailing tent at the Fort bore no such symbol, but the water-stained canvas tent isolated in the trampled

138

field exuded fear, mourning and finality. I began to look away when I passed the field and the hospital, dark thoughts replaced my innocence. Somehow this event was repressed and forgotten. Summer was clouded by the tragedy but briefly. Aunt Phoebe, turning to her usual solution, planned a picnic. We were soon caught up in the excitement of an event of quite another kind a Gypsy Camp Farewell.

The Gypsy Camp

GYPSY CAMP FAREWELL

The Gypsy Camp was the name given to the area just upstream from the pump house. Aunt Phoebe had named it. I don't believe Gypsies ever camped there, but they might have for it included the best part of the river bottom.

The pump house served as the machine shop, tool house, ice plant, and engineering center for maintenance of the Reservation at Fort Duchesne. Campbell Litster was in charge there, so it was not entirely forbidden territory to the children. Just outside the building was an old bath tub which served as a watering trough for horses. It was fitted with a standpipe of running water which was considered safe enough for a drinking fountain, although it reeked of chlorine. At that point, the river made a large bend, and through the years it had created a sandy beach and a deep pool, that had become our swimming hole. Springtime floods had deposited large trees on the sand bars long ago. One old pine was lodged in the eastern bank. Its exposed roots served as a sort of diving platform from which we jumped into the swimming hole.

Near the beach, a grassy bank was shaded by the tall cottonwoods. Bordering the beach was a bower of huckleberry bushes and wild roses that formed a secluded shelter for changing into swim suits. The Gypsy Camp was everyone's favorite spot for a picnic and a swimming party.

One afternoon, a few weeks after the U.B.I.C. debacle, we were snapping beans for supper when Aunt Phoebe said, "I think it's time for a picnic. Gene's birthday is next week. We could have a swimming party. Friday will be a good day. We can cook our supper." Of course we all agreed.

Aunt Phoebe soon had us organized into teams to do the work. The boys were sent to scout up and down the river for driftwood for the camp fire. They stockpiled it on the beach. They also cut, and sharpened willows for toasting marshmallows. The girls were set to scouring the three-legged cooking pot in which the Mulligan Stew was cooked. Girls planned the menu, even though it never varied, because it always included stew and fry bread. We also had to collect the food, and utensils needed for the picnic.

The boys retrieved the hooked tripod from the pump house and set it up over the fire pit on the beach. Aunt Phoebe offered to furnish the meat for the stew which was delivered from Wong Sing's on Friday morning. We gathered the other ingredients from the various vegetable gardens, and prepared them for cooking in Aunt Phoebe's laundry sink.

Aunt Phoebe's Mulligan Stew was famous. We had made it lots of times. Into the clean pot went a lump of butter, and then the chunks of beef. We stirred the beef until it was golden brown, then added onions, carrots, potatoes, green beans, tomatoes, seasoning, and water. We decided to have corn on the cob, since it was in season. We begged up and down the alley for ears of fresh corn. We stripped back the husks, removed the silks, and then tied the husks back around the corn cob. These were roasted by burying them in the hot ashes. We scrubbed potatoes, carving our initials in them before adding them to the hot coals to roast while the stew simmered. They never baked completely in the time allowed. Half-raw, we ate them anyway, thinking they were delicious. They smelled and tasted of wood smoke and ashes, after we peeled the charred crust away to expose the steamy interior.

On the day of the picnic, we lugged all the ingredients down to the beach, trying not to get sand in the vegetables. The older boys started the fire early in the afternoon. We hung the large pot on the hook of the tripod, and left it over the fire to simmer slowly while we took turns tending the fire, stirring the stew, and swimming.

To make fry bread, we needed a pan of yeast dough which Mama mixed for us. We carried it to the picnic, unbaked. There we took turns making fry bread. Taking a lump of dough, we stretched it into a flat cake, and then dropped it into a frying pan of hot bacon grease. The dough puffed up into a bubbly fat cake that was turned to brown on both sides. The browned cakes were lifted out with a long-handled fork and drained on brown paper.

When they had cooled enough to handle, they were dipped in granular sugar. Fry cake was a favorite treat.

Each family provided its own bowls and tin cups. Since we had no frozen juices in those days, we squeezed dozens of lemons for lemonade, and added our own sugar, mixing it all in a huge kettle. Aunt Phoebe's huge granite coffee pot was hung on its own tripod to make boiled coffee. It smelled wonderful, but tasted very bitter.

A swimming picnic was lots of work, requiring many trips from the various households and kitchens to the Gypsy Camp. Every family contributed something, even if it were only a blanket to spread on the sand. Swimming went on intermittently all afternoon while the stew simmered in the big pot.

Aunt Phoebe superintended from a special folding chair that we carried down to the beach for her. Other mothers came to chaperon, and act as lifeguards. Fathers came when the day's work was done. Supper time was announced by banging on the stew kettle with a large ladle. No one dawdled, for our appetites had been sharpened by the anticipation and exercise throughout the long hot afternoon. Supper was a marvelous communal feast. Like nearly everything at the Fort, it included whole families and all ages.

After supper we toasted marshmallows over the dying embers, taking care to avoid burning them, because they were a rare treat. The marshmallows came from Wong Sing's in little square boxes. There was much sharing and little wasting.

As the coals died down to embers, and tired bodies grew quiet, we drew the blankets closer to the fire. Aunt Phoebe's folding canvas chair became "center stage," and the evening's entertainment began. We watched Gene open her birthday presents, and then we sang to her. Then we played "Heavy, heavy hangs over thy poor head." To pay forfeits, some sang, some preferred to recite a poem, while some shared a trick, or a special event of the summer. There was lots of amateur talent in the group. Mr. Litster played his saw with a bow like a violin. Halley was very good on his harmonica. Grant, Leroy and Garth performed as a comb and washtub band. Bill played his banjo, and Bob the Jew's Harp. Sylvia and Jean danced, and Mae did acrobatic tricks. I recited a dramatic poem that I had learned for an elocution lesson in Logan. Each shared his or her talent with joy and sincerity, genuinely appreciating the gifts of those who participated.

When it grew dark, the time had come for one of Aunt Phoebe's stories. After the story we joined in community singing. Accompanied by guitar, harmonica, fiddle and a wash tub base, our songfest spread throughout the river bottom, filling the night with happiness and contentment. Our faces glowed in the dying embers of the fire. From the hills beyond the shadows of the darkened river bottom, coyotes joined the chorus that included old songs and new *The Utah Trail, Red River Valley, Moonlight On The River Colorado*, and a round or two.

Under the August moon, petty quarrels were forgotten. Shoulders and knees touched and tired eyes began to droop. With joined hands and happy hearts we sang a goodnight lullaby, bringing to a close one more perfect summer day at the Gypsy Camp. We sang:

> *Desert silver blue beneath the pale moonlight*
> *Coyote yappin' lazy on the hill*
> *Sleepy wink of lightnin' down the far sky line*
> *Time for sleepy cattle to be sti–ill . . .*
> *So now, the lightnin's far away*
> *The coyote's nothin' skeery*
> *Just singin' to his dearie*
> *Hee-ya ta-ra-la-lal-la-day*
> *So settle down ye cattle 'til the mornin'*

And so we did. Soot-stained, tired, and a bit sated, we settled down. Perhaps Aunt Phoebe was right to call us gypsies.

The Whole Gang

INDIAN SUMMERS

"They're coming! They're coming!" shouted Leroy as he clattered down the uncarpeted wooden stairs. His leather boots resounded through the empty rooms like a drum sounding the last tattoo. He raced toward the back door, skirting packing cases as he ran.

I looked up from the barrel of dishes where I was wrapping tea cups in newspaper to see why he was running. Through the curtainless kitchen window I saw a buckboard wagon, with rubber-tired automobile wheels, turn from the alley onto the lawn. A single white horse was hitched to the wagon that stopped beside our back door. Johnny jumped down, and looped his reins around the post that held our clothesline. Accompanied by three husky young men, Johnny walked toward the door. As he raised his hand to knock, my brother exploded through the doorway. Slamming the screen against the wall, he nearly knocked Johnny off his feet. Johnny laughed and caught Leroy in mid air. "Easy now," he said, setting Leroy on his feet.

Mama had followed Leroy, and she stood in the open doorway. "Hello Johnny. Everything is ready. We've been waiting for you."

Johnny swept off his black hat, revealing two long black braids fastened with red string. "Are you ready to go?" he asked.

"We'll leave early in the morning. It's a long drive" Mama said. "Your things are in here." Mama held the door open, and beckoned to the young men who followed Johnny into the back room. They were dressed in blue jeans and beaded moccasins. Like Johnny, they wore their hair plaited in two long braids. They had come for some pieces of furniture which Mother had given to Marie and Johnny. Before daybreak the next morning, my family would leave Fort Duchesne for the last time. There would be no return to the Reservation the following summer. The Alfalfa Seed Experimental Farm was being discontinued. My father's work in the Basin was finished. He would drive us to Logan to start school, and then he would return to close the farm.

I unlatched the door spring, propped the screen open, and sat down on the grass to watch. Johnny and Henry emerged from the back door carrying Mother's glass-walled china closet. They set it on the lawn, and wrapped it in a blanket before setting it in the wagon. The other two helpers carried the ice box from our kitchen, and set it beside the wagon. Next, they brought the treadle sewing machine. Last, but not least, came the most prized gift the electric washing machine! While Johnny supervised, the men struggled to hoist the heavy machine into the wagon. They eased the machine into the wagon, and Johnny tossed them a rope which they wound around the copper tub, securing it in a web of knotted rope.

Watching them load the washing machine, I recalled the time my arm was caught in the wringer. Marie was doing the washing, and I was helping. We did our washing in the large bathroom, using the bath tub to rinse the clothes. Marie lifted the clothes from the hot soapy water in the washing machine with a small length of broomstick and guided them into the wringer. I was catching them on the other side, and guiding them into the tub of rinse water as they came through the wringer. For some unknown reason I did the forbidden thing. I reached around, and tried to flatten a tangled lump of wet cloth, but my fingers were caught between the folds. The rollers pulled my hand into the wringer with the clothes. I watched my hand disappear into the wringer. Unable to let go, and too fascinated to yell, I just watched as my hand disappeared with the soapy clothes. When my elbow reached the rollers, I yelled. Marie realized what had happened, and she hit the release bar which stopped the rollers and spread them apart. I pulled out my hand, and shook my pinched fingers. Nothing was broken and no damage had occurred, but both Marie and I were shaken. Ever after, I held a certain fear of that machine, so I felt no regret as I watched them put it into the wagon. I was glad it was going to Marie, because she thought it was the most wonderful machine ever invented.

I looked at the blanket-wrapped china cupboard with regret. It lay on the lawn waiting to be lifted into the wagon, but in my mind's eye, I saw it as it had been when it stood in the parlor against the wall between the windows. The dark wood was polished and shining. Behind the glass door, the shelves were lined with doilies, their crocheted edges hanging down like lace valentines. The delicate china that my mother had painted for her trousseau was arranged on the shelves. I recalled many happy dinner parties when Aunt Mattie, Aunt Bill, Dr. Rine, and Uncle Jess came from Roosevelt. Marie always helped with those parties, letting me polish the silver while she set the table with Mama's pretty dishes. Together we spread the large white linen cloth, setting the knives, forks, spoons, and napkins in place, while Mama gathered and arranged flowers cut from her garden.

Mama remembered how Marie loved her pretty dishes. She had chosen a china bowl painted with roses to give to Marie, so that the china cupboard would not stand empty in Marie and Johnny's parlor. Together, we wrapped it in a box lined with pink tissue paper. The gift was to be a surprise for Marie. It was waiting on the big ice box in the back room until the wagon was loaded.

Though I watched the dismantling of our house with some regret, I was too excited about my future to feel sad about leaving my past. We had said goodbye to everyone at the Gypsy Camp picnic several nights before. I was relieved that there would be no more farewells, and no more annual partings from friends. I looked forward to school starting in a couple of weeks. I was going to a big Junior High School where there would be a different teacher for each class, and different classrooms for each subject. The three-storied building in Logan had a cafeteria, an auditorium with a real stage and curtains, and a real gymnasium for basketball games and dances. I would never go back to the two-room school at Fort Duchesne again.

Mama broke into my fantasy by handing me the gift-wrapped box. I straightened the ribbon bow, and waited for Johnny to finish tying the ropes. He tugged at the last knot, then turned to Mama. Taking her hand, he said, "I wish for you great happiness. I don't know how to thank you. You and Mr. Carlson have been so very good to us. We'll miss you."

"You have been very kind to us all these years," Mama said.

"Marie has earned these things. They rightfully belong to her. We shall miss you, too. Now, Virginia has something for Marie." Mama indicated the wrapped box that I held.

Johnny turned toward me, and I placed the ribbon-tied box in his hands. He looked directly at me. His dark eyes were grave as he received the gift. Our fingers touched fleetingly as we held the box between us. Children are never prepared for the consequences of their feelings, so the pain of parting struck like an arrow. My heart constricted, and I felt it would break. "Goodbye Johnny," I said, choking on the lump in my throat. "Thanks for everything. Remember. . . remember. . ."

I faltered, realizing that we were parting forever. Tears spilled onto my cheeks. I recalled being caught peering into Johnny's truck after the body of Mountain Lion was brought back to Fort Duchesne several weeks before. I felt regret and shame. Once more I wished with all my heart that Johnny had not discovered us being sly and deceitful. It hurt, knowing that my curiosity had betrayed his trust in me. I forced a smile that my heart did not feel, and raised my gaze to meet his own. I squeezed back tears, and let go of the box, leaving it in Johnny's hands as tears slid down my cheeks. I finished, mumbling, "Remember the good times."

Johnny held onto my fingers, "*Uh voo sah rah, Nah'chits.* (Farewell Little One) walk softly, stand tall and remember our good talk." It was our old and familiar way of parting. There was sadness and forgiveness in his voice. "You have a good mother and a wise father. Listen well, and your happy days will continue." His eyes brightened and he smiled, "You will come to the Bear Dance in the Spring?"

"Oh yes!" I promised. In my heart I knew it would not be possible.

Leroy pushed between us. "Goodbye, John Leroy," he said, shaking my little brother's hand as if he were a man.

"Goodbye, John Victor," Leroy answered, obviously pleased to be treated like a grownup.

Johnny turned quickly. Taking the reins, he led his horse to the alley. His friends walked beside the wagon to steady the load. I blinked to stop my tears and watched as Johnny climbed into the driver's seat of the loaded wagon. Then it moved slowly away.

"Goodbye! Goodbye!" we shouted, waving as we watched the wagon recede slowly down the alley. It moved slowly past the back steps of the house that had been Johnny's, past the green lawn, and past the cottonwood trees that shaded the grass where Johnny and I had searched for lucky four-leaf clovers. The wagon passed over the cattle guard, then paused. Leroy and I followed to the end of the alley, watching the men as they raised the heavy wooden gates of the cattle guard after the wagon crossed over. Johnny shook the reins, and turned his horse into the dusty road that circled the Fort. Johnny turned and waved goodbye, then slowly drove away. I waved back, watching until the wagon disappeared behind the hospital.

With the departing wagon, my Indian Summers came to an end. And, though I did not know it then, so did my childhood. I never returned to Fort Duchesne again while Johnny lived. The focus of my life became school, and a whole new social life in Logan. There, I grew up, and Fort Duchesne became a memory of the past. It regained significance for me when my mother died, for then there was no one to remember my childhood. I began to recreate it. I remembered the red rocks, the green trees, the endless blue sky, the open desert, the pageantry, and the sound of drums–the Indian drums.

EPILOGUE:
ABOUT INDIANS

THE LADY WHO LOVES BASKETS

Si-oo-cha-manitz, The Lady Who Loves Baskets, was her Indian name. The Uintah Band of Utes conferred it upon her with an eagle feather, when they adopted her into their tribe. I called her Aunt Bill. Mildred Miles Dillman was my mother's friend. I was often left at the Dillman home to play with her daughters Naomi, Dorothy, Mary, and "Pug" while she and Mother were busy with L.D.S. Church Relief Society activities in Roosevelt.

When I lived at Fort Duchesne, most adults were concerned with Indian affairs, but I knew no one whose interest equaled that of Mildred Dillman. As a Home Demonstrator for the Extension Service of Utah State Agricultural College, she taught classes in nutrition and domestic arts at the Reservation School at Whiterocks. Many women walked miles to attend her classes. For those who could not get to the school, Mrs. Dillman went to their homes throughout the reservation. She traded her home-making skills, and her knowledge of food production and preservation for knowledge of the Indian ways and customs. In exchange for discarded clothing, utensils, and tools of our time, she received gifts of ancient baskets, beadwork, cradle boards, buckskin clothing, weapons, tools, pipes, and drums. Those priceless artifacts included crafts of the Ute, Navajo, and other tribes. Like my mother collected fine china, Mrs. Dillman collected baskets, grinding bowls, and fine beadwork.

Mrs. Dillman's interest in Ute culture and history led her to serious studies of the ethnology, archeology, and geology of the Uinta Mountains and Basin. In the years 1929-1945, she enrolled in courses at the universities of Utah, Chicago, and Yale. In the 1930s, she began digging in the ancient settlement areas of the Uinta Basin, under the supervision of archeologist, Donald Scott of Yale. Another summer, she worked with Smithsonian archeologist, Frank H. Roberts at Mesa Verde, studying the Basket

Makers. Many of the artifacts, as well as her research and photographs, are displayed at the Museum of Man and Culture at Brigham Young University.

I went to see Mrs. Dillman in June, 1977, after many decades. She welcomed me, saying, "Oh, you were one of the *little* girls. How you have grown!" After we exchanged pleasantries, she led me to her basement, and showed me colored slides which she had collected since the first colored film became available. Selected from hundreds, they were organized as lectures which she gave regularly to school children, to camps of the Daughters of Utah Pioneers, and to others interested in the Ute culture.

As we set up the projection screen, she reminded me that it was she who had taken me to see the petroglyphs in Dry Fork Canyon of Ashley Creek near Vernal. Childhood memories rushed to my mind. I recalled being helped over large boulders, and climbing a steep hillside to the base of a vertical red sandstone wall. Figures of huge men, with square heads set upon square shoulders, were carved on the stone wall. The figures were of monstrous size. Dressed as warriors, they wore head dresses and breast plates. They carried shields and other objects. They have since become known as "The Group of Ramses II." Then, however, the petroglyphs were known mostly to sheepherders, and local farmers. Mostly they were found on canyon walls, but they were also carved and painted on large boulders found along the old trails. Many of these were gathered up, or vandalized, before preservation and interpretation were undertaken.

Projecting a slide showing a large petroglyph on a free standing rock, Mrs. Dillman paused, and pointed out that several figures had three fingers. She believed this to be the sign of Godhood. She believed those ancient people had a concept of the Trinity, and that they knew the story of the crucifixion and understood the significance of the Christian Cross. Reading the petroglyphs as hieroglyphs, she deciphered one which referred to a cross. She said she searched years for the cross. Then, following the zigzag lines on the petroglyph as a map of an ancient river, she came upon a large stone, which bore a sign pointing toward the canyon wall. Looking up, she saw a cross carved in the roof of a shallow cave which sheltered the ruined walls of a stone house. She

154

showed another large petroglyph, which she interpreted as the story of the creation. It portrayed a kneeling figure bent over a prostrate one. Outspread hands clearly showed three fingers. On the head of the kneeling figure was a long feather, at which Mrs. Dillman exclaimed, "See his eagle feather! It is spread straight back, in peace."

Changing the reel, she showed her Ute Indian friends, dressed in traditional costumes, and reenacting ancient activities and ceremonies. One portrayed a warrior mounted on a white horse. Painted for battle, he carried a buffalo hide shield, and a feathered spear. Another showed *"Nah nah Tecumseh"* seated in a cedar bark house constructed in the old manner. Beside the house was a woman wearing a sage brush skirt, bending over her baskets. She said cedar houses were used long before the elk-hide tepee. The houses always faced southwest, so the prevailing wind carried the smoke out of the smoke hole. She showed a young mother wearing a buckskin dress. The yoke and sleeves of the dress were ornamented with blue beads. She was seated on a pony, which pulled a loaded travois. The poles of the travois were used as tepee poles, and the elk hide cover supported bags of food and furs, as they would have done when the band moved from one camp to another. On her back, the young mother carried a baby in a large cradle board called a *kahn*, or little boy's house. It was beautifully ornamented with red roses worked on a solid ground of white beads. She also said, that a girl's *kahn* would have had yellow beads. Each board was unique, and was made for each new baby by its grandmother. The cradle board made it possible for women to gather food and to travel until the child was able to walk.

Mrs. Dillman said the Utes had obtained glass trade beads from the Spanish since 1500 A.D. Before that, they used quills, shells, and seeds to ornament their finely-tanned hides. She said the Indians traded beaver pelts and tanned buckskin, for beads and cloth. The cloth, was measured into lengths equal to the dressed beaver skins, and it was colorful and pliable, but never as enduring as tanned buckskins. She continued, showing me baskets of willow and grass. Each basket was shaped according to its use. All were beautifully woven from many different materials gathered from widely separated places. She showed me a very old basket, saying that when she first saw it she had protested, "The petals don't match."

"Foolish old woman, you have to let the evil spirits out!" was the response.

Besides baskets, women made elaborate bags from tanned skins for storing food. They made grinding bowls from river stones. She showed her friend, Etta Wash, grinding cracked bones into a powder from which a gruel was made to feed babies, so they would have calcium for strong teeth.

She said Indians were knowledgeable about plants, but their use of desert flowers seemed especially interesting. Two varieties of sego lily grew in the Basin. Their edible roots became a staple source of carbohydrates. They used all parts of the sunflower. Its seeds and roots were valuable sources of protein, and the dried petals were ground into flour, which was made into tiny cakes, and baked on hot stones. They ate the apples of the prickly pear cactus, and made jelly from them. They peeled the leaves to get rid of the spines, and fed them to their horses. Cactus juice was also used to clarify muddy water for cooking. They brewed primroses as a medicinal tea for treating diabetes, and other ailments. Tea made from willow leaves was used for the pain of rheumatism. Today, aspirin is compounded from the same component.

Mrs. Dillman had a superb collection of Indian blankets which were displayed on her walls, floors, and furniture. She showed me a chief's blanket, explaining that it was a genealogy chart. It was woven so that no matter how it was folded, the central design, or crest, remained whole.

I asked her about the ceremonial dances that I had witnessed as a child. She explained that the Bear Dance is the only dance indigenous to the Utes. The Bear Dance occurred in the springtime, and was originally a mating dance. The women wore special moccasins with knee high leggings. She said that only Uncompahgre leggings were attached to the moccasins. She laughed as she told how some Indians used to wrap themselves in a sheet to keep their beadwork clean while dancing in the dusty dirt floored enclosures. She explained that later, both Whites and

Indians made Bear dancing shirts from crudely painted muslin, believing they were proper ceremonial attire. She laughed again, as she told how she first went to the Bear Dance as a spectator. The Bear Dance Chief, or "the Cat," came up with a long stick, saying she must leave the ring if she did not join in the dance. Somewhat reluctantly, she joined the line of women. The "Cat" switched her bare legs each time she missed a step. Much later, the Utes presented her with an appropriate dress and leggings. It was made of white buckskin and ornamented with beads in a design created especially for her.

I asked her if she spoke the Ute language. She replied, "I spoke little Ute, but when I came to their houses, the men and boys came in from the field to be certain that their women understood what I had to say. They were such good mothers, so anxious to do everything right."

She explained that traditionally, the women educated the children until the boys were ready to be trained as warriors. On the reservation, the children were removed from the home, and sent to the boarding school at Whiterocks. It was more important for boys to attend school so that they learned English. There were pictures of children at work in the vegetable garden which was planted at Whiterocks school where she had taught. She said that the boys and girls would not work together, so she separated them. They planted gardens on opposite sides of the school, then both the children and the gardens prospered.

She showed me pictures of men using various native tools. One was an obsidian scraper about which she said, "No matter how you picked it up, it fitted your hand perfectly, so carefully had it been chipped."

She sang a lullaby for me, saying she had learned it from Old Julie, daughter of Chief Julius. As she quickly showed pictures of women at work, she named her friends who had posed for the pictures, "Francis Mountain Lion, Susy, Mary Denver, Chapoose, Marguerite, Julie. See, they are wearing my old dresses. When I was in Hawaii during the war (World War II), they wrote me from Ouray saying, 'You were so good to us, can you send us some old clothes?' Of course, it was impossible."

I wondered how she had been able to photograph so many

Indians. She explained, "They never would have treated me like this, but they accepted me as one of their own. They trusted me, and shared with me. In bestowing me with the eagle feather, they made me one of the tribe. It is a very great privilege."

As the pictures followed one after another, she said," Now here is Johnny Victor, the Indian policeman. He taught me so much!" My heart skipped a beat, for Johnny had been my teacher, too. I saw a mature man seated on a cottonwood log, but my memory superimposed another image of Johnny. It was that of a young man in beaded moccasins and eagle bonnet. He danced to the beat of a drum and to singers who sat cross-legged before a screen of willows. I said to Mrs. Dillman, "Yes, I, too, remember Johnny. He was my friend." I told her how seeing him dance had changed my feelings about Indians.

"You have forgotten," she replied, "I wrote the Pageant for the U.B.I.C. in 1934, John Victor was the principal dancer. Later, he became the Bear Dance Chief." But I had not forgotten. I never will.

We folded the projection screen, and returned to her living room. I thanked Aunt Bill for her gracious hospitality, and for sharing her knowledge of the Utes. She said, "I wouldn't do this for just anyone, but I loved your mother, and for her sake I do this for you." As we reminisced, I regretted the loss when my family moved away from people like Aunt Bill. I should have liked to share her discoveries. I suggested how fortunate she had been, she replied, "You don't think I would ignore that wonderful laboratory the whole Basin–for learning the Indian culture do you?" But so many did.

"Saturdays were my Indian Days," she continued. "They came to Roosevelt to sit peacefully on my green grass, to enjoy my flowers, to accept my hospitality. Eventually, they let me preach the gospel to them." Mrs. Dillman was a faithful member of The Church of Jesus Christ of Latter-day Saints. She said, "I believe my mission was to teach the Indians." And while she taught, she also learned.

Mildred Miles was born into a family of remarkable women. All the Miles girls were recognized for their achievements a physician, a journalist, a teacher, a scholar and anthropologist. But the degree to which Mildred developed her own talents has been insufficiently recognized. She was rare in her time. In seeking to satisfy the curiosity roused by the Indians living in the valley to which her husband had taken her, she showed uncommon diligence and integrity. While she reared a family of five children, she found time to learn about the Indians, to work among them, and to fulfill her role of leadership in the community, in the L.D.S. Church Relief Society, and in the Daughters of Utah Pioneers.

Mildred Miles Dillman was generous with her scholarship. She was a pioneer in the appreciation for Native American culture, and the need to preserve knowledge of it. She was a liberated woman, who pursued her interests with determined independence a generation ahead of her time. Also uncommon for her time, was her recognition of the role of women in the culture and lives of the Utes. Little has been written about the women. What Mrs. Dillman learned about them from her friends, the grandmothers, will be difficult to recover. But, those who would understand the power of women within the tribal structure must try. The preservation of her rare collection of Ute artifacts preserved at Brigham Young University makes it possible to share her experience.

Mildred Dillman understood the unique position of Indian women in the family, in the tribe, and in the community. As she lovingly shared her own belief with the women, she helped them acquire new skills, and greater understanding. Because she shared, many were able to adapt their lives, to acquire new skills, and to assume a new role in the twentieth century. We all owe a belated tribute to *Si-oo-cha-manitz*, a lovely lady who not only loved baskets, but the Indians who made them.

UTE CREATION MYTH

In the beginning, there were no people. Senawahv (The Maker of all Things) first made the sky, then the earth. Next he made the plants, and then the animals. Senawahv cut many sticks, and put them in a large bag. When Senawahv was not looking, Coyote came along and untied the bag, and out ran all The People. Senawahv was very angry for Coyote had spoiled his plan to give each people a place on the earth. Senawahv wanted them to live in peace without quarreling over the land.

A few people remained in the bag, and when Senawahv saw them he said, "These people will be brave people. They will be called Ute, and no one will defeat them." Then Senawahv shot his arrow high into the sky. It plowed across the flat earth, making deep canyons and high mountains. Each nation chose a different place to live. Eagle chose the mountain peaks. Bear chose the mountain caves. Deer chose the forests, and Buffalo chose the grassy plains. That is how the tribes began. It was a magic time, when animals talked.

After the People separated, the magic time ended. They began to quarrel, and to fight each other. The People lost their wisdom, and the struggle for survival began.

Senawahv had given the People a rich land, but in order to use its many resources, they had to travel through it in all the seasons. In this way, the Ute People became hunters and gatherers, and like the Bear, they chose the mountains.

"INDIANS JUST DANCE"

I remember driving home after Sunday School and I asked Mama, "Do Indians go to Sunday School?"

"A few do, I suppose. Mostly, Indians just dance."

I wonder if she knew how truly she spoke then. For dance, like other forms of folk art, is an attempt to make religious ideas visible. For Native Americans, the ceremonial dances were expressions of belief, and all members of the family participated in them. The dance that belonged to the Utes was the Bear Dance, which they danced in the spring, traditionally after the winter encampment.

Johnny Victor explained the Bear Dance to me during one of our "good talks" sometime after I first attended a dance. Many years later, I read what he said about it, after he had become a Bear Dance Chief. He was interviewed about The Bear Dance for the Duke Indian Oral History Project, Uintah School District and The Western History Center, University of Utah, published in *Ute People: an Historical Study*; Salt Lake City, 1970.

Ute Bear Dance, Uintah-Ouray Reservation, 1924
Used by permission, Utah State Historical Society

THE BEAR DANCE

Aiya, Hey, Heya!
Come Bear, Dance Bear, Dance!

Of all the Ute dances, the Bear Dance is the oldest, and it is the only one that is indigenous to the Utes as people. The Bear Dance was originally a mating dance, danced at the end of the winter encampment, and before families separated for their summer food gathering. Later, it became more of a social festival that occurred in the springtime.

The dance tells the story of a man who goes to sleep, and has a dream. He dreams that he goes to a certain place in the mountains. It is in springtime after the bears have awakened from hibernation. The man finds a bear, shuffling forward and back in a dance. The bear scratches his back by rubbing it on a pine tree, then continues his shuffling forward and back.

In the Bear Dance, the Utes imitate the movements of the Bear, shuffling forward and back. The music is made with a *morache*. The morache is a notched stick which is rubbed with a piece of bone. In olden times, the morache was made of the jawbone of the bear. The morache imitates the sound of the bear rubbing against the tree, and the drums imitate the springtime thunder which awakened him.

The ground where the Bear Dance took place was a large field, enclosed by a fence made of interlaced boughs of willows. The fence surrounded a floor of hard packed earth with an opening in one side. Opposite the opening, a shallow trench was dug. A sheet of metal was placed over the trench to serve as a resonator for the morache. Formerly the resonator was an upturned specially woven basket. More recently, wood and metal were used.

The musicians were seated around a large drum located alongside the trench. Spectators were seated along the walls of the corral. Young men and women who were going to dance, lined up in two lines facing each other. They danced toward each other, forward and back, to the accompaniment of four or five older men. The Singers played the drum as they sang in harmony. The songs were about the season of spring, which was so welcome after the cold of winter. New songs often came to the Singers in a dream, and they taught the simple melody to the dancers.

One of the Singers, called "the Cat," carried a long willow switch which he used on any shy woman's legs, urging her to dance faster. During the dance, the young woman flirtatiously flipped her shawl in the face of the man she chose. As the dance progressed, the dancers separated into couples. The dance ended when one of the dancers became exhausted and fell down. A big communal feast followed the dance.

Men and women donned all their beaded finery for the Bear Dance. Young women wore a special moccasin made of white buckskin, extending almost to the knee. They were ornately beaded, and uniquely designed for the occasion. Originally, the young men and women taking part in the dance, were indicating their willingness to accept a suitable offer of marriage.

Aunt Bill [Mildred Dillman] told me that she had danced the Bear dance, and that she had been made an honorary member of the Ute tribe. She said that any young woman who showed anxiety about marriage at any other time would have been teased with the wry comment, "See! She has on her Bear Dance moccasins."

The Bear Dance Chiefs took charge of the feast that followed the Bear Dance. They were respected elders, admired as dancers and singers, who decided when the festival should be held. They decided who should prepare the food, and make contributions to the feast. They also took charge of rehearsals and preparations of the Bear Dance arena. Sometimes a thousand people attended the Bear Dance festival. Once limited to the Native Americans, the Bear Dance festival is now open to anyone who is visiting the reservation at the time the dance is held. The festival and Bear Dance have become commercialized, so that it is more like a county fair and is a time for celebration.

THE SUN DANCE

The Sun Dance was introduced to the Utes from the Arapaho in 1902, and was danced primarily as a ceremony for the curing of the sick. Like other tribes who were hunters and gatherers, the Utes were dominated by shamans. Shamans performed their skills to heal the sick, and to direct the activities of members of small local groups. The supernatural powers of the shamans were invested in eagle feathers, eagle bones, beaded fetish bags, and medicinal herbs, all of which are important accessories to the Sun Dance.

I first went to the Sun Dance as a small child, when my parents went as guests of their close friend, Mildred Miles Dillman. She was an ardent student of Native American culture, and a trusted friend of the Utes. She fostered knowledge of their former ways, and sought to preserve this knowledge by collecting Native American artifacts and lore. I was about six or eight years of age when I first remember going to the Sun Dance with Aunt Bill, Dr. Miles and Uncle Jess. Uncle Jess Allen drove up to the Sun Dance Grounds at Whiterocks. He parked his car near the school, and then we walked through a large field of dried grass to the Sun Dance Lodge. Native Americans had come from many parts of the reservation, and were camped near the dance grounds. Their tents were clustered under the trees that grew along the river, and the dance lodge stood in an open field. It was late summer, and the grass was dry and dusty.

I remember being a little frightened as we approached the dance lodge that loomed so huge above me. The walls consisted of branches fastened to a framework of poles, so that it looked much like a large corral with a roof over it. We entered the lodge through an opening in one side, and stood against the wall. Uncle Jess lifted me up so I could see.

Overhead, the roof consisted of a large wheel made of twelve poles. The outer end rested on the low wall which surrounded the dance floor. The inner end rested in the crotch of a forked central pole, which was planted in the ground to support the twelve poles.

The sacred Sun Dance Pole was chosen by the chief, and brought to the dance ground by the tribal warriors who prepared it for the dance. Mounted near its top was a buffalo skull that represented the sun. Bundles of sage, and ceremonial herbs were fastened to the pole.

The opening to the lodge faced east, so the first rays of the rising sun would strike the Sun Dance Pole. The pole was oriented so that the sun's rays would fall on it throughout the day, drawing the sun's power to the dancers. At its base, the sacred fire pit held ashes from a ceremonial fire of cedar boughs and sage that were burned at the beginning of the dance. About half of the outer wall of the lodge was partitioned to form stalls opening onto the dance area. Each contained a willow pallet upon which exhausted dancers rested briefly.

We heard the dance music from a long way off. Its rhythm was hypnotic, and its melody unforgettable. The singers and drummers sat outside the lodge, gathered at the base of the wall. The dance had been going for three days and nights when we entered the lodge to watch the ending of the dance. I saw three or four dancers, dancing toward the pole in time with the music. They took very small steps toward the Sun Dance Pole, then without turning, danced back. Forward and back, forward and back. The steps were repeated over and over. The music never stopped, or changed rhythm. The dancer's heads were thrown back, and their eyes were fixed on the buffalo sun as they danced, forward and back.

Each dancer held a long whistle in his teeth, made from the wing bone of the eagle. A wing feather dangled from the end, and it lifted and dropped as the dancer breathed in and out. The dancers wore a long leather apron, and were naked above the waist. Their bodies glistened with perspiration. Some dancers wore necklaces of bone, or bear claws, which rattled as they danced. Some had paint on their faces and bodies. All wore an eagle feather tied in their long braided hair. It was hot, and the drums throbbed as the singers went on and on with their quavering song. The dancers moved in time with the music forward and back, forward and back. The bare feet of the dancers lifting and falling with the rhythm of the drum.

Used by permission, Utah State Historical Society

Sun Dance at Whiterocks, Utah, ca. 1930

The Sun Dance usually lasted four days and nights, during which the dancers neither ate nor drank. They were permitted to rest briefly on the pallets of willow. If a dancer fell during the dance, he was revived by the Sun Dance Chief, who lightly brushed an eagle feather over his body. The revived dancer returned to the dance, which went on and on.

On the last day, the dancers moved out of the lodge, and formed a line facing the sun. The Singers sang a closing prayer, and the music stopped.

All spectators, singers, and visitors formed a very large circle around an enormous buffalo hide spread on the ground. On it were placed offerings of blankets, beadwork, baskets, shawls, and money. The Dance Chiefs collected the offerings, and distributed gifts to the spectators, and to the guests who had contributed to the dance. The ceremony ended, and the feast began.

Solemnity vanished, and happiness, lighthearted songs, jokes, and plenty of laughter prevailed. We sat on the ground, eating chunks of venison roasted over the fire. Baskets of grease bread were passed around, followed by platters of corn wrapped in the husks, and roasted in the ashes. Trays of fresh vegetables, sweets, pinion nuts and dried berries were passed to everyone. We were served a frothy red punch made from buffalo berries, which we drank from tin cups. The festive occasion included the elders, the children, the babies, the young people, and the dancers.

After the feast, we walked slowly back to the parked cars and Aunt Bill explained the meaning of the dance. She told us it was not meant to be an entertainment. The Sun Dance was a ceremony of faith and healing. Through fasting, dancing, and song, the dancers believed that the Power from the Sun would pass to the them, and to the people who attended the dance, curing any sickness, and preventing disaster throughout the coming year. During his ordeal, each dancer experienced a vision that revealed his life's purpose. The dance was a prayer to the Holy Spirit for power and wholeness. The feast that followed was a thanksgiving for blessings received. We were privileged to be included, and though I felt anxiety entering the dance grounds, I left with my own beaded moccasins, and feeling sure that I too, had been blessed by the sun and the music.

THE LAND IS HEAVY

*"The streams, the land, and the timber upon
the mountains, you cannot take that away. These
things, they are a part of the earth and they are
heavy, you can't move them or lift them, I don't
care how big you are."*

Thus spoke Chief Red Cap when he was informed of the
Congressional Act making allotments to the Utes, and opening
the surplus lands of the Uintah Reservation to White settlement
in 1905.

When my family went to live in the Basin in 1924, the early
years of conflict had settled into an acceptance of the allotment
system, resulting in a checkerboard pattern of White and Native
American land use. The administration of Native American affairs was centered in the offices and facilities located at Fort
Duchesne. The Uintah Basin Alfalfa Seed Experimental Farm
was established on an allotment near Fort Duchesne in 1925. The
land had been leased for ten years. The Farm was operated jointly
by the Utah State Agricultural Experiment Station and the Farm
Bureaus of Duchesne and Uintah counties. My family had spent
the previous year in Roosevelt, where my father had taught in the
High School. He had graduated from the Utah State Agricultural
College with a degree in Agronomy, and planned to continue his
graduate studies while he served as Superintendent of the Farm.

I was a toddler, aged two years, when we moved into our
house at the Fort, and my awareness of our surroundings grew
gradually as I grew. My first conscious feeling about Indians, was
anxiety for I was a curiosity to them. The genetic heritage of my
Swedish and Danish ancestors was all too apparent in my blue
eyes and snow white hair. Women wanted to touch it, to see if it
were real. This made me shy of them, for their faces bending

169

close to me were solemn and unsmiling. I could not see into their black eyes to judge their motives, and when they spoke in the Ute language, it did not reassure me for I did not understand what they said. Native Americans dressed differently, and often their long dresses and shawls smelled of wood smoke and campfires.

My mother's friends, who were Native Americans living at the fort, were sometimes hired as baby sitters and part-time household help. I did not see them as different from me, but as family friends. I became aware of Native Americans as individuals as I watched them walking past the four-foot wire fence my father erected temporarily one summer to enclose our play yard. My brother and I were quarantined, because we had whooping cough. A huge orange cardboard sign was hung on the outside of the fence. It carried a message printed in large black letters, "WARNING! WHOOPING COUGH!" The practice of quarantine for communicable diseases was common in the city, but at Fort Duchesne no one had practiced it. Many persons passed by our improvised corral during that summer, when my brother and I were shunned like victims of a plague. We were often too busy playing to notice, but still we felt ostracized.

Native Americans came to the Fort in sober family groups, on solemn business. They rode in horse-drawn wagons, leaving them in the river bottom, and walking through our back yard on their way to the Administration building, or hospital. The men wore blue jeans with denim or black shirts. They wore the collar open with a brightly colored silk kerchief knotted round their neck. Northern Utes had broad flat faces, and the men wore their hair plaited in two braids that hung from beneath a broad-brimmed, black hat. The tall crown was ornamented with a brightly beaded hat band.

The women always walked behind the men. They too, wore their hair braided, but usually uncovered. Their dresses had long full skirts and they wore a large plaid blanket wrapped around their shoulders. It was secured with a wide leather belt which formed a pouch in which they carried a small child or infant on their backs. The traditional cradle board used for very small babies, was seldom seen. They always wore moccasins, sometimes ornamented with beads. The children, who were smaller versions of their parents, tagged along in ragged lines.

My upstairs bedroom overlooked the field between our house and the hospital. From there, I observed the Native Americans who occasionally came to the wailing tent located in the field beside the hospital. We children were forbidden to go inside the fenced hospital grounds, because of the contagious nature of the diseases of resident patients. We grew to fear the hospital as well as its patients, but from a distance we observed the shadowy figures who sat on the open porch which extended around two sides of the building. Many patients had tuberculosis, and some were in the last stages of syphilis, so they were thin and haggard looking.

I did not learn much about the problems of Native Americans as a child. The attitude of adults in my family was generally one of tolerance without undue concern for them. My father always felt that we were guests of the Agency, and in no position to be critical of what he considered their business. Nevertheless, I received the unspoken message that Whites were superior to Native Americans. Supervising them was the Agency's business. Benevolence was dispensed as if they were children needing direction. If I encountered hostility toward Native Americans, it was off the reservation and usually outside the Basin during the winters we spent in Logan.

During our "long talks," Johnny Victor told me most of what I learned about Native Americans. He had been sent to a special school for Native Americans and had learned about many tribes. He told me they called themselves "The People." He told me the Creation Myth of the Utes, which explained how they got their name. He talked about their dances, explaining that the Sun Dance didn't belong to the Utes. Their totem was the bear, whose characteristics they tried to emulate. The dance of the Utes was the Bear Dance. Johnny told me various myths about animals. In general, I listened to his stories much as I did the stories my Swedish grandfather told, as pastimes. I have rewritten them as I remember them, and as they pertain to my experience.

In Logan, the year I was in the fourth grade, we built a whole pioneer wagon train in the large sand table. Most of my classmates were grandchildren of Scandinavian converts to Mormonism, so it was a Mormon wagon train. When it came time to discuss the *Indians*, I tried to tell about my experience on the reservation. I tried to say that they were not bad men who attacked the white pioneers, but that they believed in the Great Spirit and held wonderful dances to express their belief. I was trying to describe the Sun Dance as a healing ritual, not a pagan celebration. My classmates jeered, and I began to cry. But, I was determined not to be outdone by their ignorance, so I finished my report by reciting Longfellow's poem "Hiawatha," which I had learned for my elocution lesson, and which they listened to, though it had nothing to do with Utes. I fled from the classroom, and took refuge in the furnace room with the custodian, Mr. Kennard, who was every child's surrogate grandfather. I never again tried to "talk" about the Native Americans in Logan.

In the general population of the Uintah Basin during the 1920's, there was one White to four Native Americans. That population included the majority of Native Americans in Utah at that time. Northern Utes seldom left their reservation for the urban areas of Utah. Leaving meant traversing formidable mountains in any direction. The roads were primitive and automobiles were not yet commonplace. The means of transportation for most Native Americans was limited to horse-drawn wagons.

At Fort Duchesne, Native Americans were always visible. But with the exception of the few families who lived within the Fort circle, Whites and Native Americans were separated by custom and residence. As a child, I was not aware of the distinctions Native Americans made among themselves. There were three distinct groups of Utes, of full-blood and mixed lineage. I did not know then that to be "full-blood" was a legal description, which determined an Indian's rights to an allotment, to water rights, and to land. I did not know that blood rights determined whether an Indian could inherit the allotments provided by treaty.

The opening of the Uintah reservation to White settlement in 1905, resulted in a pattern of ownership of the Northern Ute lands which inevitably led to conflict. Every aspect of Native American life was shattered by the reapportionment, distribution and readjustment of their vested rights to their homeland. The Agency at Ouray, which had been established for the Uncompahgre Utes, was consolidated with the Uintah Agency, and the headquarters were moved to the abandoned military post at Fort Duchesne, in 1912. There the Bureau of Indian Affairs administered justice and aid to all three bands of Utes–the White River Utes, the Uintah Utes, and the Uncompahgre Utes. A series of small towns grew up across the reservation, mostly as White settlements. This was followed by a period of canal building which made most of the reservation available for farming purposes.

The three bands of Utes on the Uintah and Ouray Reservation, spoke different dialects, and they had quite different customs and histories. The Uintah Utes were indigenous to the Uinta Mountains. The White River Utes had lived in the Colorado Rockies, and along the Yampa River. The Uncompahgre Utes had acquired the horse in Spanish times, and from their home in the southern Rockies and plains, they raided the trails to the Southwest. They had a tradition as great warriors. They were pushed into the Basin from their native lands in Colorado when silver was discovered on their lands. All lived under different treaty rights, resulting in friction among them, even before the white settlers arrived.

I gradually lost my anxiety about Native Americans. I learned to see their visits to the administration building, the commissary, or the hospital as necessary and commonplace. Their camps along the native owned irrigation canals were a familiar sight. I came to recognize many of the families living in the primitive log houses scattered throughout the reservation lands. Those homesteads were unimproved by electricity or running water. They looked poor and wretched, but no more so than those of the Basin's white settlers, who also lived in primitive log houses unadorned by paint, shade trees, flower gardens or curtained windows.

Whites criticized Native Americans as farmers, who did not care for their land. Many seemed to have no employment of any kind. No one bothered to explain to me that they lived on allotments granted in lieu of land. Many leased their land to white farmers to farm while they, themselves, worked as common laborers. It was unrecognized that the male Native American's traditional role had been totally obliterated by confining them on the reservation. The fact that he had few tools, and little skill for farming was never mentioned along with the criticism.

For the most part, I saw the Native Americans as interesting curiosities. They were colorful and exotic. Native American chiefs dressed in ceremonial regalia, rode proudly in every parade and civic celebration. The children with whom I played, and attended school, were just kids who lived in the neighborhood. Family photographs show groups of us dressed alike, grinning self consciously at the camera. Because there were so few children at the Fort, boys and girls played together, all children attended the reservation school at Fort Duchesne. Those of us who came for the summers were accepted as playmates. We often brought new toys, games, and ideas from the "city." Television had not yet conveyed culture of one tribe to the other.

When I discovered that my friend Johnny was a Native American, I was shocked with disbelief, and ashamed for the manner in which my discovery was made. I was genuinely hurt by the indifference of my elders to my feelings for him. He had been my elder brother before Leroy was born. He continued to be important to me, even after he moved from next door to one of the small cottages near the Administration building where he worked. I resented the indifference and ignorance that fostered prejudice among my wintertime peers who had no knowledge of, nor interest in, Native Americans as persons.

My father made it clear to us, that our family were guests on the reservation, and we had no right to be judgmental. He thought it best to remain silent. I was also greatly influenced by my experience and association with those persons whose stories are told in this memoir. They understood and admired Native Americans as individuals, and as a people. I learned to keep my feelings to myself, but I was forever changed by my early experience. I have felt a kinship for Native Americans, and I regret their treatment by white settlers who appropriated their lands resulting in the loss of their native culture. This feeling prompted my desire to learn about Native American life, and the culture of Native Americans. I studied their history, and read their stories. I was shocked, and ashamed, when I examined reservation documents to see witnessed thumb prints instead of signatures on vital papers preserved in the National Archives. Little had been written about the Utes that lived in the Uintah Basin when I began this memoir, so the impressions of my childhood may seem outdated today. The Native American population is much greater now, and their culture and life style is as greatly changed as that of the white settlers of the Basin. For some it must represent progress and prosperity. For others, it has been loss.

Like Chief Red Cap, I have known that we and the Native Americans are like the mountains, "part of the earth and they are heavy, you can't move them or lift them."

The land *is* heavy, very heavy it seems.

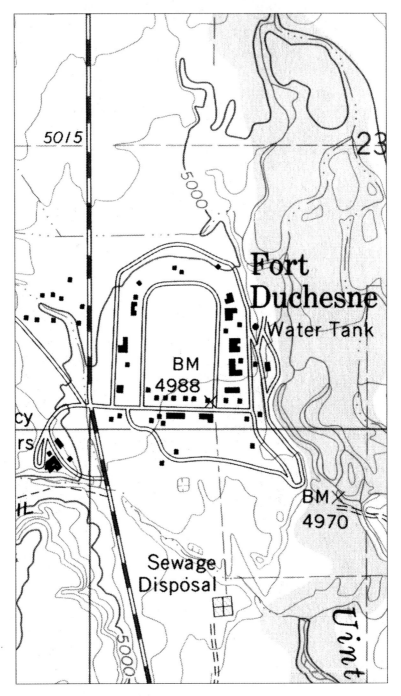

Detail of Topographic Map Fort Duchesne Quadrangle.
U.S. Department of the Interior Geological Survey, 1964.

Aerial Photograph of Fort Duchesne.
U.S. Geological Survey, September 6, 1953.
Record No. 530129. Frame No. 4736.

BIBLIOGRAPHY

PRIMARY SOURCES:
Interviews:
    Phoebe C. Litster, Salt Lake City, Utah, June 10, 1975.
    Gene Louise Litster (Mrs. Ernest Bowling) Salt Lake City, Utah, June 10, 1975.
    Mildred Miles Dillman, Salt Lake City, Utah, June 25, 1977.
    Lurrine Miles, M.D. was her professional name, but her family and friends called her Dr. Rine and her patients called her "Little Doc." She was married to Jess Allen. I went to see her in Roosevelt, Utah, June 28, 1977.
    Crumbo, Albert, Roosevelt, Utah, June 28, 1977. He ran the garage at Ft. Duchesne and was a friend of my family.

Correspondence:
    Edna Martin Paratt, Monterey, California, 1975 to 1977.
    Robert Litster, Salt Lake City, 1976 to 1977.
    Gene Litster Bowling, 1975 to 1977.
    U.S. Bureau of Indian Affairs. Letter and photocopy of news paper clipping (unidentified) sent in reply to query about Indian murders during 1934 U.B.I.C.

Archives:
    Diary; and Reports 1925-1935, John W. Carlson, Superintendent Uintah Basin Alfalfa Seed Experimental Farm. In his: Papers, Utah State University Merrill Library, Special Collections and Archives, Manuscript Collection No. 27.

    United States Department of Agriculture, Cooperative Extension Work in Agriculture and Home Economics. In: *Reports* Extension Agent Erastus Peterson, 1928-1932; Home Demonstration Agent, Alice Pedersen, 1928-1932; and Lottie K. Esplin, "Reading for the Home," 1932. Deposited in Utah State University Merrill Library, Special Collections and Archives.

Uintah Basin Industrial Convention, *Programs* for 1925, 1928, 1930, 1931, 1932. Deposited in Utah State University Merrill Library, Special Collections and Archives.

Archives of the Uintah and Ouray Indian Reservation. Photo copies of various documents, which I examined at the University of Utah, Marriott Library in 1977, while they were in the Western History Center for the Duke University Oral History Project, under the direction of Floyd A. O'Neal. (Includes photocopies of letters about peyote, marriage customs, Bear Dance, buildings and grounds at Ft. Duchesne, letters from Superintendents Kneale, Tidwell, and Page; Capt. R.T. Bonnin, Chief John Duncan, Campbell Litster and others.) (Papers were in a box labeled "Compiled Information File" 1917-1932.)

Special materials and photographs in Archives at: University of Utah, Western History Center; Utah State Historical Society Library; Utah State University, Special Collections and Archives; and Thorne Studio, Vernal, Ut.

NEWSPAPERS:

Denver Post.
Deseret News.
Roosevelt Standard.
Salt Lake Tribune.
Utah Farmer. Scattered issues, including column "On the Uintah-Ouray Reservation," 1923-1925, by Hylas C. Smith.
Vernal Express.

SELECTED PUBLICATIONS:

Bagley, Henry, "Obituary of Wong Sing" in: *Salt Lake Tribune*, Sunday, March 25, 1934, p.30.

Builders of Uintah: A Centennial History of Uintah County, 1872 to 1947; Arranged and published by Daughters of Utah Pioneers of Uintah County, Utah, 1947. Springville, UT: Art City Publishing Co., 1947.

Conetah, Fred A. *A History of the Northern Ute People*. Edited by Kathryn L. McKay and Floyd A. O'Neal. Salt Lake City, UT: Uintah-Ouray Tribe, c1982.

Coulsen and Geneva Wright, "Indian-White Relations in the Uintah Basin," in: *Utah Humanities Review*, Vol.2, No.4, Oct.1948, p.319.

Daughters of Utah Pioneers:
"Early Stores." *Lesson* for May, 1986.
"Indians and Utah." *Lesson* for March, 1978.
"Early Chinese of Western United States." *Lesson* for April, 1978.

Densmore, Frances. "Northern Ute Music;" "Mythology of the North American Indian;" "Games of the North American Indians;" in: Smithsonian Institution Bureau of American Ethnology, *Bulletin 75*. Washington: Government Printing Office, 1922.

Denver, Norma and June Lyman. *Ute People Workbook*, Compiled by Norma Denver and June Lyman, Title I Uintah School District. Salt Lake City: Uintah School District and Western History Center, University of Utah, c1969.

Fenin, George N. and Wm. K. Everson, *The Western: From Silents to Cinerama*. New York: Orion Press, c1962. "The Covered Wagon."

The Happy Homeland. [s.l.: The Uintah Basin Industrial Convention, 1925] U.B.I.C. Program, 64 p. illus.

Images In Stone; Photography by David Muench, with introduction, captions and text by Polly Schaafsma. San Francisco: Brown Trout Publishers, Inc., c1995.

The Indians, by Editors of Time-Life Books, with text by Benjamin Capps. New York: Time-Life Books [1973]. Utes. Role of Women. Cradle board. Flutes and Drum, pp. 87-105.

Jefferson, James. *The Southern Utes, a Tribal History*, by James Jefferson, Robert W. Delany and Gregory C. Thompson; Edited by Floyd A. O'Neal. Ignacio, CO: Southern Ute Tribe, c1972.

Jorgensen, Joseph G. *The Sun Dance Religion: Power for the Powerless*. Chicago and London: The University of Chicago Press, c1972.

Pratt, A.G. *Rock Art of the Uintah Basin*. 1st ed. Roosevelt, UT: Uintah Basin Standard, July, 1972.

This Is Dinosaur. Edited by Wallace Stegner. New York: Alfred E. Knopf, 1955.

Untermann, G.E. and Billie R. Untermann. *Guide to Dinosaur Land and the Unique Uinta Country*. Vernal, UT: Utah Field House of Natural History, c1972.

Utah Historical Records Survey. Inventory of County Archives of Utah, No. 24, Uintah County (Vernal). W.P.A. Ogden, UT: The Survey,1940. "Historical Sketch," pp.1-49; "The Strip," pp.34-35.

Ute People: An Historical Study. Compiled by June Lyman and Norma Denver; Edited by Floyd A. O'Neal and John D. Sylvester. Salt Lake City, UT: University of Utah, c1967.